Black Game Studies

Black Game Studies

An Introduction to the Games, Game Makers and
Scholarship of the African Diaspora

Edited by Lindsay Grace

Contributions by: Aaron Trammell and Allen Turner

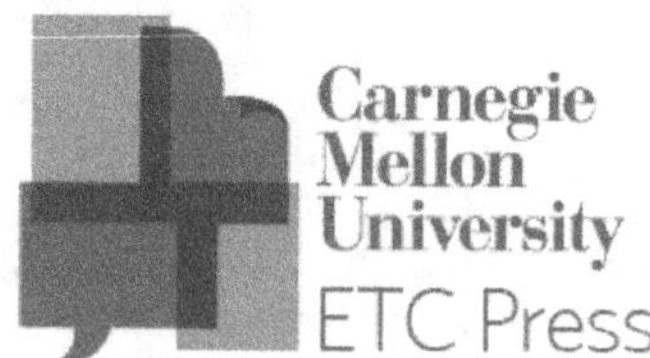

Carnegie Mellon University: ETC Press
Pittsburgh, PA

■Black Game Studies

Copyright © by ETC Press 2021 http://press.etc.cmu.edu/

ISBN: 978-1-7947-7914-3 (Print)
ISBN: 978-1-7947-7909-9 (Digital)

TEXT: The text of this work is licensed under a Creative
Commons Attribution-NonCommercial-NonDerivative 2.5 License
(http://creativecommons.org/licenses/by-nc-nd/2.5/)

IMAGES: All images appearing in this work are property of the
respective copyright owners, and are not released into the Creative
Commons. The respective owners reserve all rights.

Contents

Editor and Author ....*ix*

   Lindsay Grace..ix

Primary Contributors: ....*x*

   Aaron Trammell: x

   Allen Turner x

   Story Contributors: x

Acknowledgements:..*xi*

     With support from: xi

Section I *1*

Scholarship on Black Games...*1*

Chapter 1: *2*

An Introduction to Black Games, Blackness in Games, and Otherness *2*

   Lindsay D. Grace 2

     Games and the Game Maker Identity.......................................3

     Blackness in Games..6

     Black Games as Other Games 10

Chapter 2: *20*

An overview of Games Made by Black Game Makers *20*

   Lindsay D. Grace 20

     The fundamentals: 24

     Categorizing the Games:...25

     Games about Blackness 26

     Games about Situation: 26

     Games about Membership 26

     Games that Celebrate Culture: 27

     Games to Educate or Serve Community 27

     Games to Foster Community 28

Games about Location: 28
Games that feature Black people 29
Games that Feature Black People, but are not Made by Them 29
Games That Happen to be By Black Game Makers 30

Chapter 3: 34

Black Analog Game Designers 34

Aaron Trammell 34
Black Radical Aesthetics 36
Designing for Black Radical Aesthetics 38
Black Game Designers in the Underground 45
Designing for Radical Futures 52

Chapter 4: 58

An Autobiography of Ehdrigohr 58

Allen Turner 58
Overview 58
In the beginning 59
Days of Bungie past 66
Robots and Rampages 69
A Wide Load of Lenses 71
Return to Ehdrigohr, A new beginning 75

Chapter 5: 85

On Procedural Rhetoric and Designing Black Like Me 85

Lindsay Grace 85
Overview 85
Critical Gameplay 85
The Design 87
Conclusion 89

Section II 92

The Black Game Maker's Experience 92

Overview on Personal Narratives 93

Gordon P Bellamy 94

Neil Jones...96

They were wrong about me   they can be wrong about you.....99

Jonathan Herman Jennings 99

Boris Willis 102

On creating Home R Where The Heart Is 106

Blake Andrews 106

On Making the Run Around:.......................................108

iThrive Games Seed Institute 108

Patricia Bobo 111

Lamont A. Harrell, II 112

Section III...113

Index of Black Games..113

Alphabetical Games list by Title: 114

Aerial_Knight's Never Yield......................................116

Conquest IQ 118

Artifacts II...120

BCFX, The Black College Football Xperience....................122

Black Card Revoked...124

Black Like Me..126

Black Movie Guess Quiz 128

Blerd Domination..130

Bushido...132

Cangaço..134

Earth Cipher...136

Election Day: The Game 138

FiQuestions 140

Galactic Bar Fight 142

Healer 144

Home R Where The Heart Is 146

HTOWN FIGHT MINNIES 148

Inequality-opoly: The Board Game of Structural Racism and Sexism in America 150

Karaoke Kards 152

La Muerte 154

Objectif 156

Operator 158

Pull Your Card Music Trivia: Hip Hop Edition 160

Rap Godz 162

Rite in Rolls 164

Run Die Run Again 166

SPILL IT Card Game 168

Street Team: Reign of the Iron Dragon 170

Super High Dunk 172

Super Stick Skirmish of Superb Scrappers 174

Systemic Lives 176

The 1998 Deck 178

The Ice Cold RPG 180

The Run Around 182

The Ultimate Clap Back 184

Trading Races 186

University of Dope™...188

UnStuck 190

When I Get Free (WIGF) 192

Editor and Author

Lindsay Grace

Lindsay is Knight Chair in Interactive Media and an associate professor at the University of Miami School of Communication. He is Vice President for the Higher Education Video Game Alliance and the 2019 recipient of the Games for Change Vanguard award. Lindsay's books, Doing Things with Games, Social Impact through Design (CRC Press, 2019) and Electronic Affection: a Design Primer (CRC Press, 2020) are well received guides to game design.

His work has received awards and recognition from the Games for Change Festival, the Digital Diversity Network, the Association of Computing Machinery's digital arts community, Black Enterprise and others. He authored or co-authored more than 50 papers, articles and book chapters on games since 2009. His creative work has been selected for showcase internationally including New York, Paris, Sao Paolo, Singapore, Chicago, Vancouver, Istanbul, and others. Lindsay curated or co-curated Blank Arcade, Smithsonian American Art Museum's SAAM Arcade, the Games for Change Civic and Social Impact and others.

He has given talks at the Game Developers Conference, SXSW, Games for Change Festival, the Online News Association, the Society for News Design, and many other industry events. Between 2013 and 2018 he was the founding director of the American University Game Lab and Studio. He served as Vice President and on the board of directors for the Global Game Jam™ non-profit between 2014-2019, as the Armstrong Professor at Miami University's School of Art (2009-2013) and on the board for the Digital Games Research Association (DiGRA) between 2013-2015.

Primary Contributors:

Aaron Trammell:

Assistant Professor of Informatics, University of California-Irvine

Allen Turner

Professional Lecturer, DePaul University, Founder/Creative Director of DePaul Originals Game Studio and Owner/Designer of Council of Fools LLC

Story Contributors:

Blake Andrews (Everythingistaken), Gordon Bellamy (Full Professor, USC Games, CEO, Gay Gaming Professionals), Patricia Bobo Senior Vice President of Operations, Cards for all People), Lamont A. Harrell II (CEO & Founder of Black Game Maker's Association) , iThrive Games SEED Institute , *Jonathan Herman Jennings* , Neil Jones (Aerial_Knight) , Boris Willis (Associate Professor of Experimental Game Design at George Mason University and Founder, Black Russian Games)

Acknowledgements:

The editor would like to thank each of the game makers and their representatives who contributed to better understanding of the work. Importantly those who shared their personal stories are doing more than sharing – they are offering others a glimpse into their lives. I'd also like to acknowledge student mentees and assistants, Caleb Solomon (Brown University) and Casey Ann O'Brien (University of Miami) for their work in proof-reading the book. Final thanks to the many organizations who helped promote or otherwise support this project, including the new Center for Global Black Studies at the University of Miami and the Black Game Maker's Association. Lastly,

With support from:

Higher Education Video Game Alliance (HEVGA) , Black Game Maker's Association (BGMA) and the University of Miami School of Communication

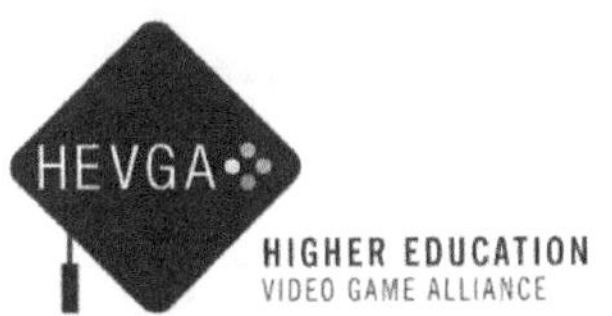

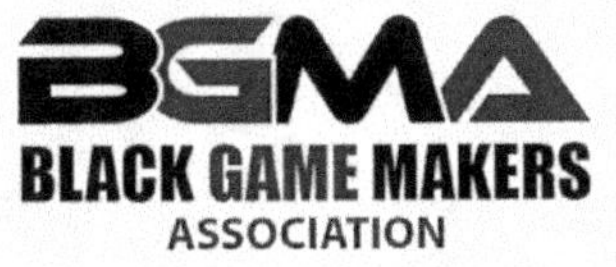

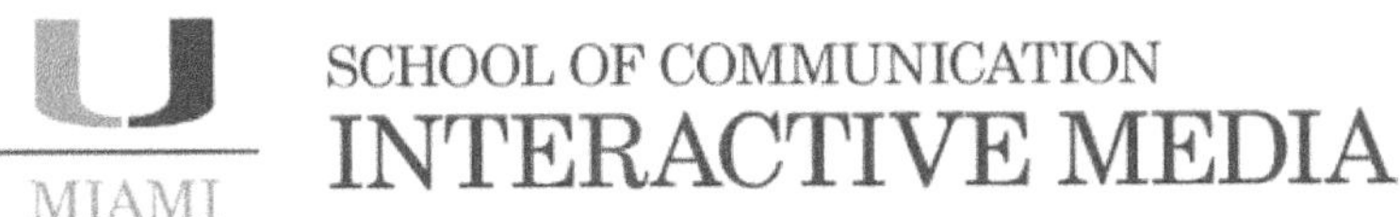

Section I

Research on Black Games

Chapter 1:

An Introduction to Black Games, Blackness in Games, and Otherness

Lindsay D. Grace

It is unnecessary to state that the work of Black game makers is under under-researched. It is a statement so plainly obvious that it need not be said at all. This book aims to help move the research forward, even if in a small way. This is by no means a comprehensive resource, but instead the product of a variety of community outreach and research. It is hoped that this is the start to something more. It is aimed at providing a single starting point in the relative void of research examining and showcasing games made by members of the African diaspora.

As such, this book defines Black widely. Although much of the work collected here comes from members of the African American community, diasporic works are not ignored. The complexity of racial identity is far greater than this work aims to examine. It simply aims to be inclusive of a general Black community, its culture and those who self-identify. It is work organized and edited by a member of its community, for the communities that benefit from such work.

While this work is largely focused on games, contextualization in race, its history and its dynamics may be useful. The myriad of texts on the topic are too many to list in these few pages. Instead, it may be useful for readers examining the wider contexts to review collections that aim to serve a similar purpose across other media. Bearden and Henderson's History of African American Artists 1790s to Present (1993) and White and White's The Sounds of

Slavery: Discovering African American History through Songs, Sermons, and Speech (2005) are good places from which to begin positioning this work. Likewise, Field's The Emergence of African American Film and the Possibility of Black Modernity (2015) provides a kind of sense of activity and momentum potentially analogous to games. Like the more comprehensive books on other media that preceded it, the work aims to catalog and curate. It takes the work of Black game makers as one trajectory for understanding the community, its work. It is a way of highlighting the cultural, artistic, and educational value of such games.

Games and the Game Maker Identity

In the contemporary, identity is perhaps even more wed to game design than it has been in the past. We, as players, researchers and designers have come to the point of recognizing the media as more than consumer product created by an amorphous, anonymous, or abstract corporate factory. It is of course easily argued that this was never really the case. Consumer and precipitously, player behavior has shifted toward not only evaluating the product but the characteristics of the company, people, or person that made it.

Game companies and other makers have been increasingly responsive to the consumer awareness that a product is perceived not only by what it is, but under what terms it was made. In the physical world, this guides the decision to buy ethically made products instead of those that exploit local communities or that employ sweatshop labor. In the digital world, this is represented by the growing concern over organizations that violate standards for equal employment and equitable workplaces. As of the writing of this book, one of the most notable cases is the 18 million USD settlement by Activision-Blizzard for US Equal Employment Opportunity Commission (EEOC) violates (Diaz, 2021). In such an environment, some socially conscious consumers wonder about such events as they consider their next purchase of a Call of Duty or Candy Crush game.

It has become common to ask the question of who, when asking the what about a game. Where once a player would ask what they might do in a game, they are also asking - by whom was it made? This shift in consumer behavior, gives more fuel to the need for academic research that leads with the question - who made this and how? Examples abound from the player who seeks a game made by women developers, a researcher studying queer games, or a designer who integrates their indigenous heritage overtly into the work they do. In this milieux there are a variety of books on queer games, including Queer Game Studies (Ruberg and Shaw, 2017) and Video Games Have Always been Queer (Ruberg 2019). There are also researchers like Dr. Elizabeth Lapensée doing work to support both indigenous game makers and integrate elements of their culture into game experiences.

Then there is the reality of Black games. There is some research into race in video games (Everett & Watkins, 2008). There is even the well-researched "Virtual Census: representation of Gendered, race and age in Video games" (Williams, Martins and Consalvo, 2009). There are the historical examinations of African games from social science perspectives (de Voogt, 2001) and collections of African indigenous play (Burnett and Hollander, 2004).

What is missing, is a collection or analysis of Black game makers in the contemporary, particularly within digital games and popular culture? By analogy, there is work in mining the history and identity of Blackness in Africa, but far less work on the African-diaspora's contemporary. By another analogy, there is evidently more work in repatriating the cultural artifacts of indigenous African culture, than examining, celebrating, or even identifying its modern contributions. The pastiche of studying Black games looks more like the African savannah and Egyptian pyramids, than the modern metropolises of Nairobi or Atlanta.

■ Black Game Studies

The easiest example of this is in the academic study of the ancient game of Mancala. Mancala is a game of probable African origin (Culin, 1894) and commonly recognized board game past-time for the African diaspora. It stands as the single most researched and documented game in the literature of African-diaspora games (save for some professional sports analysis). Mancala as subject to the *games in culture hypothesis* is rightly under critique as unproven (

The problem with the abundance of Mancal research, is of course, that a single game, a game from the continent's oft-emphasized history, fails to capture the work occurring off the continent and more importantly, in the now. Much like identifying blackness with a history of spears and drums, such monolithic work belies the richness of a culture. In its worst it stereotypes, reducing the value of cultural contributions to a few emblems that confirm unhealthy notions. Failing to appreciate the contemporary can read that the best is behind, instead of ahead. That Black play is best understood as stones counted across an ancient board.

Yet in the contemporary, as the 19th century fascination with the game of the African content recedes, so too does its prejudices. In the 21st century researchers like Mkondiwa (2020) puts into question the accuracy of the games in culture hypothesis. The hypothesis is part of a persistent line of thinking that claims mancala playing cultures are advantaged by such play toward being better at business practices. Likewise, Alex de Voogt, Misconceptions in the History of the Mancala Games examines the historical evidence to "dispel a long-standing belief that so-called complex societies are more likely to play strategic games" (2021). In that analysis, are some hints at a larger, problematic, and perhaps systematic tendency. The tendency to want to see monolithic pattern, to make a general case of a diverse group, or as we more commonly put it – stereotype. While it may not be true that Mancala research demonstrates the stereotype of Blackness in games, it is evident that contemporary research unearths century-long assumptions that seem uncomfortably similar to cultural understanding in other domains.

The problem is understanding one for the whole. It's in failing to comprehend or study the diasporic nature and seek a simple, convenient understanding of a complex ecosystem. Saliently, de Voogt sets out to question "the status of mancala games as a group that shares a common history."

This problem in Mancala, is also a problem in understanding Black games. It is a problem in understanding women's games, queer games, indigenous games, Nordic games, or anyone group's games. It's the problem of wanting to find pattern, where pattern may not be. To link correlations to causations. To think, that there is a comprehensive guide to a community or to assume there are quintessential examples of an ever-evolving space.

The problem of Mancala, if it can be framed as such, is also demonstrated in the research's slowly antiquating line of thinking. A line of thinking, that has routes in a colonial history valuing the person who absconded the artifact, over the people who produced it. One that saw a hero in a tomb raider. A culture that sought the one secret treasure that unlocked some knowledge, provided access to a mystical power, and gave dominion over others. Such myths don't fade away quickly, but instead need a critical light and repeated inquiry to ebb away.

This book is designed to work toward a more productive and equitable future. One that does not place the name of the family who donated the African mask to the exhibit, but instead seeks to highlight the artist who made it. An approach that takes a broad look at Black games and the people who make Black games. It does so by cataloging the work, analyzing the work, and by offering self-report by game makers.

Blackness in Games

Defining Blackness is a complex of diasporic history constructed, destroyed, and reconstructed by a variety of researchers and pop-sociologist alike. While readers might find substance in definitions provided by literary review by Nguyen and Anthony (2014) and the critical philosophy of Molten (2008), it's most important for this work to start with the simplest of definitions. Work borne by or through communities who cultural, ethnic, or genetic history ties to Africa. This perhaps follows more closely the historical one-drop rule (Khanna, 2010) than necessary, but functions as a means for starting such work.

One of the most common themes on the literature of Blackness is the push-pull between the multiple identities defining Blackness. Nguyen and Anthony frame black authenticity as "commodifying realness and legitimating membership" (2014). Their use of commodifying is in itself useful for both its reference to the history of people traded as commodity, but also as a sense of barter that occurs in demonstrated blackness. There are the outward signs of blackness, both genetic and purchased, but these are balanced by the actions that legitimize membership to any of the diasporas many communities. In short, wearing a dashiki does not guarantee identity nor guarantee acceptance into the community of West Africans, just as having curly hair and dark skin does not assure Black authenticity to some diasporic groups.

Although this should be obvious, it's worth noting that the same can be said for a game. Featuring people of color, does not make it a game for people of color, just as wrapping a game box in African green and gold make it more authentic. Such efforts may actually do the oppositive, emphasizing their inauthenticity in choices that are ignorant of authentic blackness (if such a thing exists).

Molten's earlier work further complicates this, by introducing the pressures applied to the Black identify by historical, philosophical, and pseudo-scientific perspectives. There is no still moment in Blackness. There is a perpetual call and response or dance that responds to negative and positive forces. As molten frames it, "this strife between normativity and the deconstruction of norms is essential not only to black academic discourse, but also to discourses of the barbershop, the beauty shop and the bookstore" (Molten, 2008).

The challenge with Black games in this context is the space between normativity and the deconstruction of norms. It is important to note that there is no readily apparent avant-garde of Black games. Through this research it is clear that unlike other communities of identity within games and allied creative work, there is neither a canon of defining work nor a defining opus. When compared to the literary fields, where early anthologies like Black Poetry (Randall, 1988) were created in a time of black solidarity, there does not exist a comparable collection, clearinghouse, or compendium.

How then does the work of a game find its space between the normal Black game and the others? The short answer is in dialogue with other media. Lacking enough markers to the edges of Blackness in game design, much of the work is in itself a kind of avant-garde. It is work that new, unusual, and experimental because it is the outlier the crowded world of games.

Another way to consider it is to see the communities of Black game makers as the center of that which defines black games norms. These are communities, which ebb and flow in their impact, activity, and contributors. There are social media groups, panels, supporting organizations and other pop-up communities that support the Black identity in games.

Yet, when compared to other creator identity driven work of game makers, Black game making is under-documented, under studied and under-celebrated. This is not an observation meant to align one game identity against another, but instead to note the inequity. An iniquity that may be as much fed by the geographic and cultural centers of digital game making, as by larger systemic issues.

The reasons for these differences obviously have multiple sources. There's the fundamental underrepresentation of Blacks in the games industry (Hackney, 2017), a challenge that has been often described but rarely addressed in substantive and effective means. There's the economics of game making, which until the relatively recent rise of indie game making in the digital space relegated low-cost design to analog solutions (e.g., card games and board games). Likewise economic disparity in the US and the many other regions where racism exists, also contributes to the technographic limitations. For digital games these technographic limitations include access to the technology, a fluency with it, a network of peers to support interest in it, reliable internet connections, the hardware to produce digital games and a variety of other elements that many experienced game professionals take for granted. In the non-digital games space, limitations in access to the finances, business models, promotion networks, support communities, and related challenges in access make the seemingly low barrier to entry in analog game design higher.

This leaves one unmentioned reality that needs to be highlighted: racism. This is not to say that the games community is actively engaged in thwarting Black game makers, but instead that in the wake of the industry's growth, Blacks seem to have been left behind. Despite being a substantial proportion of game consumers, participation in game making has been far more limited (Grace, McCaskill and Scott, 2018). By the International Game Developer Association's survey estimates, Black people represent less than 2% of the game making industry (Weststar et al, 2019).

In report from some Black game makers interviewed for this project, the resounding theme was that such designers and developers simply didn't feel there was a space for them.   For some they arrived with the skills, with the creativity or software skills, but could not fully enter the community of game makers. This is of course a challenge that many new to the industry may feel, as there are often more people looking to enter the industry than opportunities.

Yet, among the growing embrace of independent games this is also surprising. Why is it that members of the Black identity struggle to find their space in the larger game making community? This is not a question easily answers. Instead, it provides an opportunity to ask the question critically. What are the factors that contribute to this disenfranchisement? What is the result of this exclusion? How can it be better corrected? The answer to some of those questions are alluded to in the personal reports and individual game-making efforts of the examples in this book. They are evident in the need to own Blackness in games, to define, sometimes in opposition to the history of less-than desirable portrayals of Blackness in games. They are also evident in the independence of game makers, in their efforts to start something new and sustainable.

The space of game making is full of a variety of identities. Just as Blackness is not one thing, Black games are not one specific set of attributes. They are instead an evolving space between normativity and it's opposite. They are, at lease for the time being, an avant-garde from an underrepresented identity.

Black Games as Other Games

One of the most interesting and perhaps most alarming realities is the development of games about the Black experience by people who are not of the black diaspora. Beyond creating the games with the stereotype often derided by researchers, there's something noteworthy about such activity. Why are such games being made by people not of that identity, and why aren't they engaging with Black game makers to do so? Logically it should be acceptable to make such games without members of the identity, as stories and games about women have been created by men for millennia. Yet, the result of those creations can be disastrous, awkward, and offensive. Hence the admitted need for feminist literate and feminist games.

In cinema, the reported dearth of Native American or Hispanic actors created the gateway for olive skinned Caucasians to play those roles.

■ Black Game Studies

In reality, there was no dearth of people to act the roles of their identity, but there was certainly a myriad of systemic societal structures that made such individuals too far to reach. This is perhaps another contributing factor to the shortage of talented game developers and designers to help develop games with a Black voice.

By considering this historical precedence we can start to see what may be happening in the game industry at large.

In these contexts, it is likewise interesting to think about how much the culture of game making has often been about a distinct kind of otherness. The culture of game making has often been a central part of its own avant-garde. Through the years it has embraced the games industry as a place for smart, different people to do unprecedented things. This culture is apparent in an aesthetic that champions died hair, adopted mononyms, game inspired pseudonyms, and is often looking for something new and different.

The irony of this advice is not lost in a book about Black game makers. For a person of color, they wear their distinctness in the industry often. It is sometimes common to be the only readily identifiable person of color in roundtables, for example.

What then does it mean to be an obvious other in a community that both champions otherness and seems uncomfortable with it? More accurately, what does it mean to participate in a community that is reluctant to become comfortable with your otherness?

Identity has increasingly become an important part of the culture of the game making community. It has, of course, been met with substantial tension, as some view identity politics as unnecessary in games community. The most notable of these rejections culminated in Gamer Gate (Todd, 2015) and persists in those who continue to believe it's shifting values. But anyone who critically and logically analyzes any claim that games are not about identity is likely thinking too shallowly.

Games, especially digital games, have profited from championing the identities games allow players to experience. The most profitable games let players be a science fiction soldier, lead an armada, play coach to a professional football team, or be a strong tomb-raiding woman. To say that games are not about identity feels tantamount to claiming that film is not about lens and perspective. These may not be the only elements, but they are certainly important.

The claim that games are not about identity is often used as a way of covering over the relatively limited identities available in games and their compliments (Kafai, Cook and Fields, 2010) as well as the lack of diversity in the industry.

This is further complicated by the tensions apparent in representation. As players take on the identity of their oversized Black male character in a fighting game, eager to take the best parts of the stereotype and leave its racist history behind. As molten writes, "blackness has been associated with a certain sense of decay, even when that decay is invoked in the name of a certain (fetishization of) vitality" (2008). One potential fantasy in game making may be the illusion that stereotypes (not archetypes) can be at once invoked from media history and detached from their alarming literal histories.

The Black stereotype in games is fantasy at its finest and perhaps also its most uncomfortable. It is a moment of using Blackness, without owning Blackness. That is, it is enjoying the benefits without any of the responsibility. It is a way of employing or invoking the metaphorical, Black card, without accepting the rights and responsibilities therein. It can read as a way of doing providing the minimally viable product, a representation of Blackness, as substitute for invigorating the work with authentic Blackness. To some it may play as the Cigar Store Indian has, an offense to both the ceremonial use of tobacco and image of the noble savage caricature. Our contemporary society is well aware of the power of images, portrayals, representations and their history. New media

12

scholars will likely also recognize the relationship of reality, simulacra, and simulations (Baudrillard, 1994).

Of course, this detachment from the reality of experience pervades games and is not distinct to race. It is apparent in the ways we depict war, often failing to accept its responsibilities. Its apparent in the way we depict histories and a myriad of other realities. Games are not bereft of problematic simulations, from the lived experiences of World War 2 to the dynamics of hegemony.

But it's worth noting that every medium that has done so in the past, had a reckoning. The Disney catalog is not without it's now censored racist characters. Films once heralded as masterpieces are now seen as abominations. So too, will some games.

In the meantime, it seems essential to catalog the work of this particular other. It is important in support of future work that might bemoan how little was done. It's important as a means of preservation of culture. It's important as a way to allow a peek inside a much more substantial world than the surface reveals.

It may prove to be one of the great ironies of the industry's growth, but analysis demonstrates that all of the racial identities Blacks are the more supportive of games than other groups (Lenhart, 2015). The Black community is, by this perspective, responsible for the industry's commercial success. It is of course ironic, that its participation in that successes is not reflected.

It useful to remember that members of the Black diaspora disproportionately represent some of the nation's greatest professional sports play, and their college equivalents, but few see long-term sustainable benefit from their contributions (Powell, 2007). That is, while there are many black game players, there are fewer in management. This leads to the often a team member, rarely a quarterback scenario. Black game players abound, but Black game makers are rare. Black game executives perhaps even rarer.

It is a situation that uncomfortably parallels slave history in the North and South America. Black slaves helped make the financial success but saw none of the profits. The dearth of eSports athletes (save for Fighting games tournaments) as well as the limited participation in the industry only complicate this.

The production of games by Black game makers represents a shift from being sold, to owning. They represent cultural production, instead of cultural consumption. It is a shift from being sold the images of Blackness, to owning how Blackness is framed among players. It is a move away from accepting what is given, and instead toward making what the community wants.

As Nielson wrote in their 2018 report:

> *"African American consumers no longer see their virtual actions as distinct from "in real life behavior," which has empowered their adoption of digital platforms to affect real-world change. While Black consumers are still voracious consumers of digital content, this influential demographic has increasingly leveraged the democratization of digital platforms to become prosperous content creators. Thus, African Americans are no longer content being thought of simply as voracious consumers; they want to be known for the influence they've always possessed, as the creators they've always been. "*

Nielsen's widespread analysis may very well be trickling into the game industry. An industry, that struggles, like other tech sectors to recruit and retain one of their biggest consumer bases (Curtis, 2021).

None of this critique is provided to detract from the industry. This critique is not provided out of a disdain or lack of love for the industry. Instead, it is provided for just the opposite. I love this industry. I love it enough to have dedicated half my career to it. I love it enough to praise it and to tell it when it's making a mistake. With love comes responsibility - a responsibility to care, appreciate and respect. This book serves as an opportunity to help the game making community grow, reflect, and improve itself.

It might also strike readers that when referring to the Black community the letter B is capitalized. This is by design for multiple reasons. While it is an easy shorthand for disambiguating the people from the color, the primary reasons are connected to the realities of ethnic identity. As the Chicago Manual of Style suggests, "names of ethnic and national groups are capitalized" (2021). The Columbia Journalism Review provides a substantive analysis and argument for this use (Laws, 2020).

Hence, it is used as a way of distinguishing the proper noun of Black made games, from others. Yet another reason is found in the art-historical precedent of Dada, Situationists or other notables in the understanding of contemporary art and new media. These are names for collections of ideas, experiences, philosophies, and related intersections of practice. So too, it could be argued, are Black games. Black games, also rest at the intersection of a notable and distinct intersection of ideas, experience, philosophies, social and communal realities. Black games are borne from a distinct creative movement, by which the capitalized word signifies unity.

This sense of unity is important in the all-too-common apportioning of Black games and of Blackness as other. The creation of Black games does something essential. It offers the opportunity to subverts the conventions of dominating ideologies by simply being. Instead of emphasizing the dichotomy of otherness, there is an opportunity to complete the whole. It is an opportunity to complete the missing puzzle, to make whole what is not and balance that which has tipped too far in one direction. It offers another side of playing in my world, living in yours (Leonard, 2003). It creates an opportunity to play in our world. A world diverse, vibrant, complex, and carried by a chorus of voices.

References

1. Bayeck, Rebecca Yvonne. "A review of five African board games: is there any educational potential?." Cambridge Journal of Education 48.5 (2018): 533-552.
2. Bearden, Romare, and Harry Henderson. A history of African-American artists: From 1792 to the present. New York: Pantheon Books, 1993.
3. Burnett, Cora, and Wim J. Hollander. "The South African indigenous games research project of 2001/2002." South African Journal for Research in Sport, Physical Education and Recreation 26.1 (2004): 9-23.
4. Cain, Curtis C. "Beyond the IT Artifact-Studying the Underrepresentation of Black Men and Women in IT." (2021): 157-163.
5. Chicago Manual of Style, Chapter 8, Section 38, last accessed October, 2021, https://www.chicagomanualofstyle.org/16/ch08/ch08_toc.ht ml
6. Culin, Stewart. Mancala: The National Game of Africa. US Government Printing Office, 1894.
7. de Voogt, Alex. "Mancala: Games that count." EXPEDITION-PHILADELPHIA- 43.1 (2001): 38-46.
8. de Voogt, Alex. "Misconceptions in the History of Mancala Games: Antiquity and Ubiquity." Board Game Studies Journal 15.1: 1-12. 2021
9. Diaz, Jaclyn. "Activision Blizzard Strikes An $18 Million Deal Over Its Workplace Harassment Lawsuit", September 28, 2021, National Public Radio, https://www.npr.org/2021/09/28/1041068091/activision-blizzard-strikes-an-18-million-deal-over-its-workplace-harassment-law
10. Everett, Anna, and S. Craig Watkins. The power of play: The portrayal and performance of race in video games.

MacArthur Foundation Digital Media and Learning Initiative, 2008.

11. Grace, Cheryl, Andrew McCaskill, and Mia K. Scott-Aime. "From consumers to creators: The digital lives of Black consumers." The Nielsen Company (2018). https://www.nielsen.com/us/en/insights/report/2018/from-consumers-to-creators/

12. Grace, Cheryl, Andrew McCaskill, and Mia K. Scott-Aime. "From consumers to creators: The digital lives of Black consumers." The Nielsen Company (2018). https://www.nielsen.com/us/en/insights/report/2018/from-consumers-to-creators/

13. Hackney, Elizabeth. "Eliminating Racism and the Diversity Gap in the Video Game Industry." J. Marshall L. Rev. 51 (2017): 863.

14. Kafai, Yasmin B., Melissa S. Cook, and Deborah A. Fields. ""'Blacks Deserve Bodies Too!'': Design and Discussion About Diversity and Race in a Tween Virtual World." Games and Culture 5.1 (2010): 43-63.

15. Khanna, Nikki. ""'If you're half black, you're just black": Reflected appraisals and the persistence of the one-drop rule." The Sociological Quarterly 51, no. 1 (2010): 96-121.

16. Laws, Mike. "Why we capitalize 'Black'(and not 'white')." Columbia Journalism Review 16 (2020). https://www.cjr.org/analysis/capital-b-black-styleguide.php

17. Lenhart, Amanda. "Chapter 3: Video games are key elements in friendships for many boys." Pew Research Center: Internet, Science & Tech 6 (2015). https://www.pewresearch.org/internet/2015/08/06/chapter-3-video-games-are-key-elements-in-friendships-for-many-boys/

18. Leonard, David. "Live in your world, play in ours: Race, video games, and consuming the other." Studies in media & information literacy education 3.4 (2003): 1-9.

19. Mkondiwa, Maxwell. "Mancala board games and origins of entrepreneurship in Africa." PloS one 15.10 (2020): e0240790.

20. Moten, Fred. "The case of blackness." Criticism 50.2 (2008): 177-218.
21. Nguyen, Jenny, and Amanda Koontz Anthony. "Black authenticity: Defining the ideals and expectations in the construction of "real" blackness." Sociology Compass 8.6 (2014): 770-779.
22. Powell, Shaun. Souled Out?: How blacks are winning and losing in sports. Human Kinetics, 2007.
23. Randall, Dudley. The black poets. Bantam, 1988.
24. Ruberg, Bonnie, and Adrienne Shaw, eds. Queer game studies. U of Minnesota Press, 2017.
25. Ruberg, Bonnie. Video games have always been queer. NYU Press, 2019.
26. Stenros, Jaakko, and Markus Montola. "Nordic larp." (2010). https://trepo.tuni.fi/handle/10024/95123
27. Todd, Cherie. "Commentary: GamerGate and resistance to the diversification of gaming culture." Women's Studies Journal 29.1 (2015): 64.
28. Weststar, Johanna, Eva Kwan and Shruti Kumar, International Game Developer's Association Developer Satisfaction Survey (2019) https://s3-us-east-2.amazonaws.com/igda-website/wp-content/uploads/2020/01/29093706/IGDA-DSS-2019_Summary-Report_Nov-20-2019.pdf
29. White, Shane, and Graham J. White. The Sounds of Slavery: Discovering African American History through Songs, Sermons, and Speech. Vol. 2. Beacon Press, 2005.
30. Williams, Dmitri, Nicole Martins, Mia Consalvo, and James D. Ivory. "The virtual census: Representations of gender, race and age in video games." New media & society 11, no. 5 (2009): 815-834.

Chapter 2:

An overview of Games Made by Black Game Makers

Lindsay D. Grace

This chapter is provided to support a general understanding of the state of Black game making in the 21st century. It is not meant as a comprehensive analysis of the games produced by the diaspora. Instead, it offers a snapshot of information volunteered through members of the community and collected through game studies research. It provides an introduction to the characteristics of games produced by members of the community to help frame an understanding of the practice. In much the way a film studies student might read about the defining and unique characteristics of Russian Film, Chinese media or women film makers, this work aims to provide a starting point from which any student, researcher, or practitioner might begin to understand a diverse and rich space.

Much of the work in aggregating such sources relies on either the marketing potential of being featured as a game maker or in the support and access to resources that develop from such fellowship. That is, the work is aggregated for commercial gain or to support opportunities for profit. The goal in this work aims to do something more. While the practical benefit of financial capital is valuable, the long-term archive, identification of cultural capital has its benefits too. Increasing the awareness, understanding and significance of this work helps include it in the cannon of essential creative work and to push toward the foreground the values it champions. This chapter aims to help archive the work for academic study and cultural documentation.

■Black Game Studies

The chapter contains a content analysis of 50 games by Black game makers. It functions as a broad overview to provide relative comparison and illustrate patterns. It also aims to help describe the catalog of games made by Black game makers through identifying the general attributes of them. It is not meant to stereotype or define these games, but instead to provide a starting list of characteristics that may both capture distinct elements of the practice and provide fodder for future debate.

Ideally this analysis also provides foundation for other researchers examining the characteristics of media provided by distinct identities. The patterns described here can likely be compared to the work of other communities to examine shared and disparate characteristics. This work aims primarily to report, not analyze.

There are many methodologies to conduct such research. This analysis was informed in part by prior content analysis conducted by this researcher on games that share either character (Grace, 2013) intent (Grace, 2010), or content (Grace and Haung, 2020). There are a variety of approaches to doing such work well (Krippendorff, 2018), with the one caveat that the domain is admittedly thinly researched.

Instead of conducting a formal content analysis this work employs a combination of survey, self-report, and interpretation. In much the way someone like Brian Sutton Smith sought to understand play activities in his contemporary (Sutton-Smith, 1959), this chapter aims to provide a snapshot of a space that is undoubtedly ever-changing.

Initially, this research began with a wide call to submit games produced in part or wholly by members of the African diaspora, globally. This call was shared across social media, direct email, email-lists, formal academic presentations, and through the informal networks of the African American community. These included broadcast to the official Digital Games Research Association

(DiGRA) community, the Blacks in Games (BIG) Facebook group, the Higher Education Video Game Developer's Association (HEVGA), and the Black Game Maker's Association (BGMA) electronic and in-person networks. All invitations and calls were provided in English only. Games were also added to the original data set through research documenting the racial identity of the game-makers. These included news reports from Black Enterprise and other publications.

39 Games were submitted by the game developers themselves or their representatives as part of the general call. An additional 11 games were identified through public media and published research. This means the bulk of the data presented in this analysis is derived from self-report and must be interpreted as such. When possible, the work was evaluated to verify its relationship to the African diaspora, the play experience, and distribution. Completing the set to a round 50 games provided a statistically simple collection for sampling and extrapolation.

As is the case with all such research, more time, more examples, and more detailed analysis are always valuable. At odds with this goal is the need to document and analyze this work before it dissipates from online stores, runs out of stock, no longer works with contemporary hardware or otherwise becomes unavailable. Anyone who has done this kind of work recognizes the myriad of challenges in documenting play and designed play experiences. In this space in particular, limited budgets, deprecated software (e.g. Adobe Flash) the need to perpetually update hardware and software, and the culling of low volume sales software on app stores all create accelerated expiration dates. Archiving such work is no longer merely an effort in saving digital files on redundant drives, but also means using snapshots of old operating systems and emulating software environments that are no longer available. It also means photographing and playing analog games multiple times to capture elements not obvious about such games.

The value of capturing the practice, documenting it formally, and offering summary of patterns is not only valuable to those who seek to understand it, but also as a means of preserving an element of the culture. Games are often subject to the same spirit of consumption and discard that plague other media. To help avoid the fate of now destroyed pulp fiction, graphic novels, and even the rarest of baseball cards, this work aims to capture a few dimensions of the work while they can still be studied.

It remains obvious that when games are understood as something cultural, as something more than the mere single experience of playing them, their value and the value of understanding and preserving them becomes extremely evident. Many an historian has bemoaned the challenge of interpreting the ephemeral. These are oft-cited challenges of documenting and understanding cultures for which the archive of relevant media is intrinsically not durable. This is the challenge presented in documenting that which is transferred through oral tradition or coded in the ever-evolving dialects of colloquialism. This is the challenge that sometimes plagues the analysis of cultural others, whose networks, values, and means of communication differ from the standards of the dominant cultures that archive them.

Games too are obviously subject to this same challenge. Their colloquial dialects are software dialects, their oral tradition equivalent is apparent in the yellowing playing card and the out-of-print board game. The goal in this work is thus to stave off that inevitable decay, which is accelerated by both the wave of new media offered for consumption and by the persistent atrophy of aging digital product. While nothing replaces play, but play, documenting and analyzing the content of this play should at least allow for some sense of the tradition. Just as famous paintings were once touched, we also recognize that seeing them from behind the glass of the museum helps. In the least such display offers on opportunity to experience them while also preserving them. In this basic content analysis, and the subsequent catalogue, it is hoped that some of the history of this work is preserved.

The fundamentals:

The most basic distinction between these games can be made between those that require computing hardware to play (e.g. digital games) and those that do not. Analog games, or those that require no computing hardware, represent 31% of the games analyzed. The remainder, or 69% required computing hardware of varying complexity.

In the analog game category, there were 6 board games and 14 card games. Of the digital games, 48% were available as computer games (i.e. Windows, Mac O/S or other non-mobile operating systems), 19% were mobile games, 16% were console games, 10% were designed for Virtual Reality, Augmented Reality or mixed reality. The final group, web only games, comprised 7% of the games studied.

These digital game classifications indicate the primary mode of play, as some digital games were offered in more than one platform. When determining the primary classification, a mix of the self-report, highest installation number by platform, and complete versus trial version availability were used. If a game offered a web-only trial, but offered a complete Windows PC install, it would be classified as a computer game, not a web only game.

38 games were created by a single person from the community or by a team of people who identify as Black, Indigenous, People of Color (aka BIPOC). 7 Games were created only in part by a person belonging to the African American Community. 5 were created through a participatory design process working with members of the African American community.

■Black Game Studies

The earliest work was created in 2007 the newest in 2021 (the year this work was conducted). The mean release year was 2017, with most common date (aka mode) of 2020 and a median of 2018. The data set admittedly may lean toward the most recent releases as game makers are more actively marketing, advertising, and engaged with communities when the game is new or recently released. This reality should temper any interpretation that might conclude a blossoming practice in the last decade or a peak production date in 2017 or 2018. These dates are provided simply to provide a sense for the era from which the content analysis was conducted.

The data set is also primarily focused on North American game-makers, as 47 games analyzed were made in the United States or Canada. The remainder were a game named Earth Cipher (Media Breeze, 2021) developed in Tanzania, and two games, Bushido (On the Table, 2019) and La Muerte (Casa do Goblin e Sherlock SA, 2018) by Brazilian game developers.

For the 4 games ranked and distributed on Steam (https://store.steampowered.com/), the mean score was 81%. These games were Tiny Bird Garden at 93% (Super Retro Duck, 2017), Hex Gambit at 78% (One Man Left Studio), Treachery in Beatdown City at 77% (NuCHallenger, 2020), and Combat Core at 73% (MABManZ, 2016).

It is also worth noting the funding models for these games. Some were funded through crowdsourcing, such as the $16,568 USD raised for Earth Cipher. Others, operate through print on demand services. Most commonly for digital games, they rely on open markets like Steam and mobile app stores.

Categorizing the Games:

Such analyses are typically most useful when contextualized within some pattern. The following general categorizations are provided not as an ontology, but instead to demonstrate patterns relevant in the data set. It is not the aim of this work to determine a specific game categorization schema, but instead to provide a pattern from which further work can be explored. As may be evident, these are not mutually exclusive categorizations.

Games about Blackness

Obviously, a genre of games about Blackness exists within the games studied. These games vary in their focus but typically refer to the experience of being black in specific contexts (e.g. Being Black in America) or the character of Blackness. As the maker of Systemic Lives (2020) states, "this game is specifically about blackness in America, and how blackness still plays a part in determining outcomes for people's lives."

Games about Situation:

Similar to games about Blackness, which can be understood as being about the situation of Blackness, games about situation offer a perspective on a dimension of the maker's situation or a subject situation. Situations in this context might be the situation of categorizing race and the role specific philosophies or values assert themselves as conflict (e.g. being a woman in a sexist world, being a person of color in a non-diverse environment). Inequality-opoly, who's tag line reads "The Board Game of Structural Racism and Sexism in America" (2016) is an accessible example of this design pattern.

Games about Membership

Games about membership employ play to acknowledge or explore knowledge of the black culture, experience or prescribed racial identity. They typically rely on in-group knowledge to play successfully. Where a trivia game might rely on shared collective knowledge, games about membership attempt to winnow the required knowledge set to the community's shared or defining characteristics. The most obvious example of this is Black Card Revoked (CFAP Holdings LLC, 2015).

Games that Celebrate Culture:

Other games aim to celebrate the culture of the community, noting quite appropriately that games can function as a vehicle for sharing and discussing elements of culture. These games rarely employ complex procedural rhetoric (Seiffert and Nothhaft, 2015), but instead use culture as topic. The most common focus is some element of popular media, such as Hip-Hop culture or movies. The popular card game University of Dope (Vance Hall LLC, 2016), the mobile game Black Movie Guess Quiz (Cincy Quiz, 2019), and The 1998 Deck (Ordinary Genius, 2015) are all prime examples of this. In the self-report and descriptions of these games there is often an emphasis on preservation of knowledge, a rejection of status-quo (i.e. the Black community needs its own version of …) or an emphasis on the opportunity to celebrate past success.

This is distinct from games that seek to teach cultural attributes or change culture, which are more aptly attributed to games designed to educate.

Games to Educate or Serve Community

Where games that celebrate culture might seem to be education tools, they are distinct from games that aim to impart and assess knowledge. Such games often aim not only to remind players of past histories, but to expose them to new knowledge as part of play. In classical educational game design some games act as assessments, others provide knowledge delivery. The games to educate or service community tend to lean toward providing knowledge and may secondarily rely on some form of assessment.

These games may also aim to encourage productive conversations for synthesizing new knowledge or otherwise generating change. The deck of financial conversation cards in FiQuestions (Financial IQ, LLC, 2020) is an example of this. The makers of the game indicate, "Financial IQ's FiQuestions card game asks 69 thought provoking questions to help people build their financial IQ" as a means of sparking new conversations about money.

Games to Foster Community

Almost a permutation of games about membership and that celebrate community, games to foster community aim to build community through play. They often employ a premise that requires collaborative problem solving or supportive work. The SPILL IT Card Game (2019) is a good example of this. As the game marketing materials explain, it's a "card game that sparks authentic group discussion while getting tipsy in the process." The aim is the kind of bond that structured play supports.

Games about Location:

Just as there are games about Blackness, there are games that take the community identity of a location as their focus. These games are often about situating identity by location, over other attributes like skin color or cultural origin. They do so sometimes as a way of marketing the unique character of the game, sometimes to share the distinct character of the location, other times as a combination of celebrating culture, determining membership or imparting situation. The easiest example of this is FarRock Dodgeball (Side B Gamingm 2021).

Arguably, games about subsidized housing, the colloquial hood, or predominantly Black neighborhoods might read as games about location. In the data set, many such games, however, use these locations as backdrop to other themes or as a focus of a game more about situation than location.

Games that feature Black people

Just as a location may be featured in a game, the obvious existence of games that aim to feature Black player characters, non-player characters, or people of color characterizations are a reasonable categorization. Appropriate to the tradition, some of these games simply apply the situations, mechanics, and related attributes of predominantly non-Black games toward Black depictions. They do what the Cosby Show (Havens, 2000) did to prime-time television, by depicting a familiar formula with a new skin tone. The easiest example of this, Treachery in Beatdown City (NuChallenger, 2020), abounds with Afro-centric depictions ranging from its president Blake Orama (an anagram-like transliteration of US president Barack Obama) to its varied player and non-player characters. Interestingly, in the game's satirical play, is a plethora of situational conflict that makes the game also about situation.

Another example exists in BCFX: The Black College Football Experience (Nerjyzed Entertainment, 2007). It is a sports simulator featuring Historically Black Colleges and Universities (HBCU) and their players. This, however, aims to do more than merely feature the players, it also showcases and celebrates culture by providing a virtual museum of HBCU football and provides playable half-time shows.

Games that Feature Black People, but are not Made by Them

This category is perhaps the most awkward. While the history of games is littered with racist depictions and awkward attempts at diversifying characters, there exists a category of games that depicts Black people without any input from the Black community. The worst of these stand in infamy and include the African Dodger carnival game and more recently Ghettopoly (Chang, 2003).

While neither of these games were part of the analysis, its important to acknowledge this categorization. Most notably because these games have profited from Blackness. Ghettopoly, in particular, was distributed at Urban Outfitters retail stores and while resulting in a lawsuit, continued to leave it's developer wealthier than many of the game-makers featured in this book. Perhaps more alarming, the game continues to rise in value retailing at $99 USD, likely due to its limited supply and perhaps an apparent thirst for such an experience.

Games That Happen to be By Black Game Makers

The last useful characterization is perhaps the most important. A variety of games are made by members of the Black community that are not explicitly designed for, about, or in service of the Black community. There are, unsurprisingly, games made by members of the African diaspora that are not explicitly about an aspect of Blackness. This is not to say that such games are not inspired or shaped by the creator's experience or culture. Instead it is important to acknowledge that not everything made by Black people is about Blackness.

It is a point that need be made primarily in the context of in-group, out-group politics. It is also a point that needs to be made in environments that expect people of color to do the work of representing an entire community through their individual work. The work of making games is challenging enough on its own and there are game makers who aim to make regardless of identity. One of the logical fallacies that often arises in these contexts claims that if it is not about or designed for the community, than it does not belong in the community.

This logic fails in several ways. First it limits the work of community members to that which is bound to Blackness. It tethers the work to Blackness in ways that are unproductive.

Second, it fails to recognize that all cultures are a product of interplay between that which is aimed at them and that which is not.

Lastly, it fails to allow for a productive future in which a game is enjoyed by its experience, not the color, creed, or identity of its maker.

References:

1. BCFX, The Black College Football Xperience. 2007. Nerjyzed Entertainment. Xbox 360.
2. Black Card Revoked. 2015. CFAP Holdings LLC. Analog game.
3. Black Movie Guess Quiz. 2019. Cincy Quiz. Android Mobile.
4. Bushido. 2019. On the table. Analog game. https://www.ludopedia.com.br/jogo/bushido
5. Combat Core. 2016. MABmanZ. Windows PC. https://store.steampowered.com/app/405670/Combat_Core/
6. Earth Cipher. 2021. MediaBreeze Multimedia. https://www.earthcipher.com
7. FarRock Dodgeball. 2021. Side B Gaming. Windows PC. https://store.steampowered.com/app/1364240/FarRock_Dodgeball/
8. FiQuestions. 2020. Financial IQ LLC. Analog Game. https://fiquestions.com/
9. Ghettopoly. David T. Chang. 2003. https://boardgamegeek.com/boardgamedesigner/2776/david-t-chang
10. Grace, Lindsay and Haung, Katy. State of Newsgames 2020:A snapshot analysis of interactives, toys and games in journalism and allied industries. JournalismGames.com, Miami, Florida. July, 2020
11. Grace, Lindsay D. "A topographical study of persuasive play in digital games." Proceeding of the 16th International Academic MindTrek Conference. 2012.
12. Grace, Lindsay D. "Affection Games in Digital Play: A Content Analysis of Web Playable Games." DiGRA Conference. 2013.

13. Havens, Timothy. "The biggest show in the world': race and the global popularity of The Cosby Show." Media, Culture & Society 22.4 (2000): 371-391.
14. Hex Gambit, 2018. One Man Left Studio. Windows PC.
15. https://sites.google.com/view/inequalityopoly/home
16. Inequality-opoly. 2016. Board Game.
17. Krippendorff, Klaus. Content analysis: An introduction to its methodology. Sage publications, 2018.
18. La Muerte. 2018. Casa do Goblin e Sherlock SA. Analog Game. https://www.ludopedia.com.br/jogo/la-muerte
19. Seiffert, Jens, and Howard Nothhaft. "The missing media: The procedural rhetoric of computer games." Public Relations Review 41.2 (2015): 254-263.
20. SPILL IT Card Game. 2019. SPILL IT Card Game: https://www.spillitcardgame.com/
21. Sutton-Smith, Brian. "The kissing games of adolescents in Ohio." Midwest Folklore 9.4 (1959): 189-211.
22. Systemic Lives. 2020. Digital Day Dream. Windows PC. https://digitaldaydream.itch.io/systemic-lives
23. The 1998 Deck. 2015. Ordinary Genius, LLC. Card Deck.
24. Tiny Bird Garden, 2017. Super Retro Duck. Windows PC. https://tinybirdgarden.com/
25. Treachery in Beatdown city. 2020. NuChallenger. Nintendo Switch.https://www.nintendo.com/games/detail/treachery-in-beatdown-city-switch/
26. University of Dope. 2016. Vance Hall LLC. https://www.universityofdope.com/

Chapter 3:

Black Analog Game Designers

Aaron Trammell

It's 1965 and The Avalon Hill General, wargaming's premier magazine, features a Black man on the cover. He is the limo driver of Elwood Gardner, one of the company's representatives, and he poses with Elwood and a huge bag of money for a publicity stunt. It's 1980 and two dark skinned heroes surround a dragon on the Cover of Dragon, hobby role-playing's premier magazine. Two months later, Dragon includes a black high school student in a depiction of a school yard and three months after that a black student on the cover participates in a food fight with his peers. In 1982, The General features a Caucasian rendering of Cleopatra on their cover. It wasn't again until February 1995 that Dragon would feature a Black character on their cover—again a pair of evil Drow [dark/Black] elves, killing an adventurer. On the fan circuit representation was not much better. It wasn't until Alarums & Excursions #40, the main fanzine of *Dungeons & Dragons* interest that a Drow elf was featured on the cover. And in the thirty year timeline covered here, there were no more instances of Black people on the covers of any of these three publications. Hobby games, as such, were largely packaged, sold, and presented to their audiences as a space of white cultural production. Even as moments of integration came and went through the American popular consciousness—Black cool and multiculturalism—for the most part hobby games insulated themselves from these conversations by marketing only to a specific and niche set of consumers.

The tragedy of this story, both then and now, is that Black people have long been active as designers in what I refer to as the analog game scene—a scene comprised of the common interests of role-playing game, card came, board game, pervasive game, and live-action roleplaying game fans (Torner, Trammell, and Waldron, 2014). Take Mike Pondsmith, for example. Pondsmith was designer of the 1987 tabletop role-playing game *Cyberpunk 2013*, a game that has now become somewhat of a franchise, yielding most recently CD Projeckt Red's *Cyberpunk 2077*. Even though *Cyberpunk* was a cult hit, big enough to influence the development of the AAA video game title forty years later, Pondsmith's race is barely visible in the game itself—and why would it be? In film and theater the Non-Traditional Casting Project (Willis, 1992) was only just beginning to advocate for a more inclusive approach to casting in the mass media. Pondsmith was publishing for a postal network of predominantly white hobbyists at a time when hobby role-playing games were only really available at model train stores. Pondsmith, of course, wasn't alone either. There are many other Black designers in the hobby game scene.

This chapter surveys the work of Black analog game designers in order to show how central, inspirational, and innovative Black design practices are to the creative space of game design. While Black designers of digital games are addressed elsewhere in this book, the aim of this chapter is simply to amplify the exciting projects that Black designers have been a part of, thus arguing against a deficit perspective which asserts that Black designers haven't been adequately involved in analog games. Although the history of the hobby game scene has been predominantly white, Black designers have long worked on non-digital games. Not only have these designers been there all along, so to speak, but they have set the creative stage for a present boom in Black design in today's hobby game scene. This Chapter proceeds by genre to discuss Black analog game designers so as to better discuss and describe the exciting projects in which these designers have been engaged.

Black Radical Aesthetics

Perhaps Frantz Fanon said it best when he wrote, "Not only must the black man be black; he must be black in relation to the white man" (Fanon, 2008, 82-3). Here, Fanon is referring to the significance of colonization to the construction of Blackness. Blackness, as an identity or as a lived experience exists insofar as it is the result of years, decades, centuries of subjugation and struggle. Indeed, it is the brutality and violence of colonization that pulls the inequity of Blackness into focus and which has long been a common point of solidarity between Black and Brown people worldwide. This book is about Black game designers who are either African or part of the African diaspora in descent. This focus is intended to shine a light on developers from a particular history of minoritization (Crooks, 2019, 119), and in doing so speak to the unique conditions of Blackness globally.

It must be said, then, that by adopting this focus in this chapter I do not mean to belittle, reduce, or minimize the experiences of the broader coalition of BIPOC game designers who have also endured abuse, harassment, struggle, and dehumanization as they work to make their excellent games. Far from it. I write about Black game designers from Africa and the African diaspora because it helps to refine my analysis and highlights how these designers are part of what Hortense Spillers terms a "rupture" in African culture. She writes, "The massive demographic shifts, the violent formation of a modern African consciousness, that takes place on the sub-Saharan Continent during [the start of] the Atlantic Slave Trade in the fifteenth century of our Christ, interrupted hundreds of years of black African culture" (Spillers, 1987, 68). Contending with the aesthetic, social, and narrative impact of the fissure described by Spillers means sketching the contours of an artistic scene that has endured in spite of hardship and across space. A scene which knows itself by virtue of this history more even than the folks in it know each other.

■Black Game Studies

Fred Moten calls this aesthetic sensibility "the break." For him it's essence of the Black radical tradition. It's a recognition that Black radicalism demands holding on to contradictions--embracing both the horror and the hope of Black artistic expression. Moten is, of course, describing music, Abbey Lincoln's scream in Max Roach's improv improvisational "Triptych: Prayer/Protest/Peace." Here Lincoln sounds "troubled by the trace of the performance of which she tells and the performance of which that performance told" (Moten, 2003, 22). Is Lincoln in pain or is she exuberant? She's both and neither. She is the scream; she doesn't own the scream; she's just performing the scream; she is more than a scream. Moten's theorization of Black radical aesthetics is indebted to the W.E.B. DuBois's double consciousness—where one is always evaluating themselves through the eyes of white society (DuBois, 1994, 5). Black artists constantly pull this duality into their work. Their work is radical, because they are radical. The survival, perseverance, and success of Black people in cultures that have been colonized and defined by white Europeans is itself a radical form of expression.

The Black radical tradition applies to more than just music, and so in this chapter I look to analog games to consider how it is articulated in design communities today. As I note in the introduction, this is a far more radical intervention than one might at first think. By and large Black people are largely absent from the publicity and concept art of many early hobby games. I argue elsewhere that this is because the hobby game scene was mainly the invention of white suburban men (Trammell, Unpublished Manuscript). This barrier to entry imbues each analog game from a Black designer with a unique sense of struggle, compromise, and purpose.

The aesthetic output of Black game designers *is* varied and that itself is the contradiction of Black radicalism within the analog game scene. While some designers like Chris Spivey and Julia Bond Ellingboe (who this chapter will discuss in greater detail later) make explicit overtures to Black history in their work, others like Eric Lang subvert by playing with popular culture and remixing historical narratives from the Nordic countries, East Asia, and even fantasy worlds. Analog games as a design category overall sit across many genres and each of these genres has a different consumer base, different distribution network, and even different design conventions. Knowing how to speak to, with, and between these different sensibilities speaks to the skill of the designers this essay catalogs in the sections that follow.

Designing for Black Radical Aesthetics

Eric Lang is one of the most popular board game designers working today. Until 2020 Lang was the Director of Game Design for Cool Mini or Not, a board game design company that specialized in light miniature based wargames with broad market appeal. Many of Lang's games focus on adapting intellectual property into an exciting board game experience. The list of properties Lang has played with is impressive: Marvel, Game of Thrones, Star Wars, The Godfather, Dilbert, and more. One of Lang's greatest talents as a designer is being able to imagine how wildly different worlds and settings might be transformed into a board game. In this regard, Lang is the master of the remix.

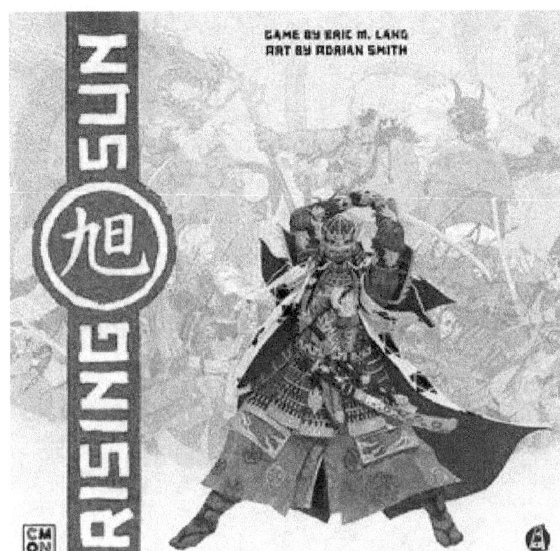

Figure 1 - The Cover Art of Eric Lang's Rising Sun.
Image labeled fair use by publisher CMON Limited.

Lang's creative output constantly reimagines and reforms the presuppositions which we players bring to the game table. Games in his "Mythic trilogy" of wargames are prime examples of this. *Blood Rage* (2015) takes Norse mythology and innovates a wargame where part of the goal is to kill your own troops and send them to Valhalla. His game *Rising Sun* (2018) takes place in feudal Japan and has a heavy focus on the economic consumption of war. And finally, the third game in the trilogy, *Gods of Egypt* (forthcoming) pushes players to contemplate religious dogma. In it players take on the role of gods in a polytheistic pantheon competing for followers in a world that is turning to monotheism for religion. All of Lang's games in the trilogy allow players to toy with relatively large miniatures that represent monsters from the various mythologies.

Black Radical Aesthetics inhabit Eric Lang's designs in how he subverts conventions of the wargaming genre to bring in more fantastic elements from cultures on the margins. Although Lang's game designs appropriate and repackage a variety of mythologies (Norse,[1] Japanse, and Egyptian), he uses these mythologies to recenter minoritized cultures in a genre that all too frequently

---

[1] I do not think Lang is making a statement about race and minoritized culture in the game *Blood Rage*. Instead, I think Lang was using the rich mythology of Nordic culture to design a game that would make his design work legible to a community of largely White hobbyists.

fetishizes the history and symbology of white men.[2] Games in this trilogy are all wargames, a genre that this chapter has already pointed to as being notoriously White in how it is represented by the companies and designers who have historically produced these games. By appropriating many conventions of the wargaming genre, but then reskinning these games with themes that dive deep into Japanese and Egyptian mythology Lang is making space for stories to be told in these games that vary the celebratory accounts of Robert E. Lee, the Confederate general, and Erwin Rommel, the Nazi general's military prowess.

---

[2] I recount a short history of Avalon Hill and TSR Hobbies' magazine covers earlier in this chapter to help make this point. Another excellent example of a typical attitude toward representing BIPOC People in wargames games is the atrociously titled book by Phil Eklund in his simulationist game Pax Parmir, "In Defense of British Colonialism." Pax Parmir is about indigenous communities being played against one another by colonial rule. Here Eklund writes, "British rule was more stable than the weak, corrupt, and capricious regimes they replaced. Both India and Afghanistan had suffered from centuries of battles between petty warlords. But in India, British rule brought a century of peace, marred only by the localized 1857 Indian Mutiny. Upon Indian independence in 1947, the end of Pax Britannica immediately sparked the Tamil separatist movement, as well as an endless series of Indo-Pakistani wars and conflicts. Since both countries now have the bomb, the next war could be nuclear, with dire consequences for the world." Eklund's description highlights the degree to which some designers still view the culture of BIPOC people as barbaric and in so doing continue to frame Western European culture as that which is "civilized," thus presuming that all others are barbaric. You can find this excerpt from the Pax Parmir rulebook here:
https://playthesethings.files.wordpress.com/2018/11/pax_pamir_excerpt.pdf

Returning to Mike Pondsmith, his design of the *Cyberpunk* franchise speaks well to Black Radical Aesthetics as well. *Cyberpunk* is special insofar as it is a paradigm case in how Black designers are able to subvert the expectations of their readers and play against genre conventions. The tagline of 2019's recently released sourcebook *Cyberpunk Red* (2019) reads "The Roleplaying Game of the Dark Future." The future is dark, namely, because Pondsmith articulates a dystopic vision of a future where

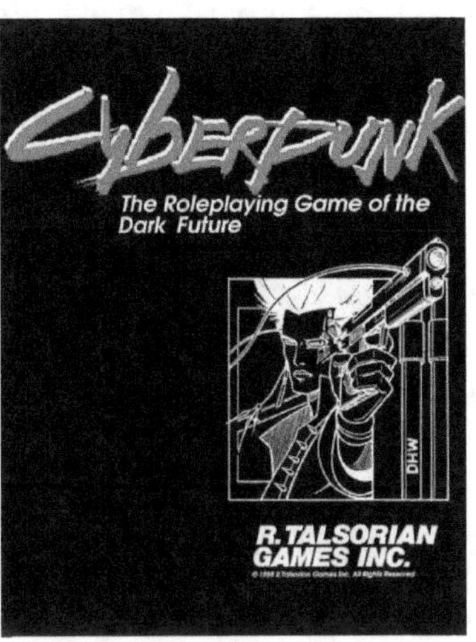

Figure 2 - Cover of the early *Cyberpunk 2013*. Image used for purposes of critique.

corporations run amok, people have found new drugs to tune in and drop out with, and the hustle of urban life is contrasted only against life in the bombed out wastelands that surround "Night City." The future is also dark because the future is Black. "Night City" is minority White and the world is, in many ways, imagined from a perspective that takes Black culture for granted and works to make the exotic mundane.

The break is still present, it lingers in every detail of the world, and has even drummed up some controversy in the game's digital adaptation, *Cyberpunk 2077* (2020). Some critics of Pondsmith's work have suggested that the game furthers racist stereotypes by uncritically presenting BIPOC characters in a gang called "The Animals." Pondsmith's response: "Who the fuck do YOU think you are to tell ME whether or not MY creation was done right or not?"(Robinson, 2019) perfectly captures the essence of Black radical aesthetics. Pondsmith refuses to be told what Black is, and how Black can identify or disidentify. As a black author Pondsmith is vocalizing against the double standard by which his work is being judged. "The Animals" are at once too Black, and not Black enough. But Pondsmith inhabits the break. He knows that Black art isn't always legible by White folks and he eagerly embraces these contradictions in his design.

Julia Bond Ellingboe's role-playing game *Steal Away Jordan: Stories From America's Peculiar Institution* (2007) is a game about slavery in America. The game is best described by one of Ellingboe's collaborators, Katherine Castiello Jones in an interview with Ellingboe. Jones writes:

For those readers who have not yet played the game, *Steal Away Jordan: Stories from America's Peculiar Institution* is a tabletop role-playing game in which players tell the collective stories of enslaved people. Written in the spirit of neo-slave narratives like Margaret Walker's Jubilee, Toni Morrison's Beloved, and Octavia Butler's Kindred, the game is set during the United States' antebellum period. Each session focuses on the struggles of a group of slaves to achieve their secret goals. These range from large goals like killing the overseer, to smaller goals, such as keeping a family member from being sold away, learning to read in secret, or getting a pair of shoes. Players have to work together to achieve their goals, but the game also forces characters to make hard decisions about when to prioritize their own goals over the needs of other characters. Does one make a break for it during a moment of conflict or stand up for another slave as they are interrogated about missing goods? (Jones, 2016, paragraph 2)

Steal Away Jordan focuses on the retelling of American slavery. By drawing on the work of Black authors to think through how living through slavery implies managing trauma, scraping by, and even conspiring with one another toward the ends of freedom, comfort, and even joy, Ellingboe expertly shows how Black radical aesthetics can inform the role-playing game genre.

Often Ellingboe's critics would describe *Steal Away Jordan* pejoratively as something that wasn't a game. It was critiqued as being an educational exercise. Some people were "afraid to play it" (Jones, 2016, paragraph 16). Specifically, some even related to Ellingboe that they were "afraid of getting it wrong" (Jones, 2016, paragraph 17). In other words, because Ellingboe focuses so specifically on the institution of American slavery in her game, the threat of an experience of play that touches on trauma as opposed to pleasure was too much for

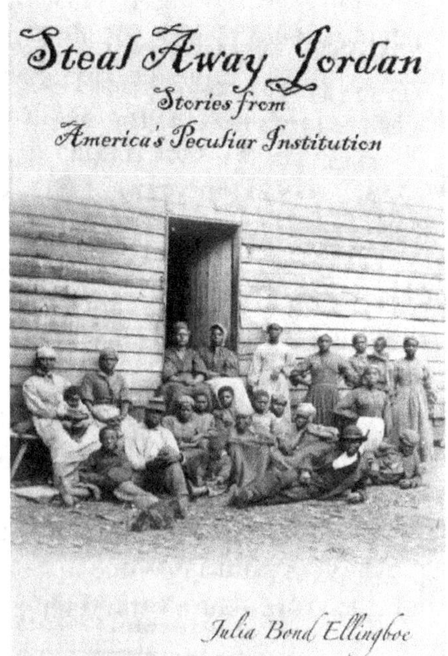

Figure 3 - Cover art for Ellingboe's *Steal Away Jordan*. Image used for purposes of critique.

many of the presumably White players who encountered it. "The definition of 'fun' is something that gets policed," Ellingboe recounts, "There is an idea that games have to be fantastical. That a game shouldn't make you think beyond what pleases your character" (Jones, 2016, paragraph 23). But this is life in the hold. We're just holding on to the things that make us Black. The indelible mark that we all carry with us that replaces a sense of origin with a common cause and solidarity.

Embracing the painful as well as the pleasurable is what makes Black radical aesthetics so poignant. If Frederick Douglass had omitted Aunt Hester's scream in his Narrative in the Life of Frederick Douglass, would it have inspired so many to work toward abolition? Would the flourishes of John Coltrane be so sublime if he didn't play with notes that were both tonal and atonal in organization? As Ellingboe has so adeptly put it, the Western European canon of play scholars polices affect. It polices what José Estaban Muñoz terms the depressive position—an angst shared globally by BIPOC people that relates to our shared traumas, histories, and oppression under global capitalism (Muñoz, 2006, 675). Thus, sharing the pain of Black fantasy is an important part of the project of Black radical aesthetics. There is a political end to this work, of course. As André Carrington puts it, "Haunting will not go away so long as its conditions of possibility remain intact" (Carrington, 2016, 23).

The policing of play that allows for pleasure and not pain is one of the many things which generates the conditions of possibility which allow trauma, death, and pain to haunt Black aesthetics. Although Ellingboe, Lang, and Pondsmith all take different approaches to their game designs, a through-line of the Black radical tradition runs through the work that all three have published. Within each corpus of work lies a desire to surface and make legible the contradictions of White culture. Pondsmith imagines Black futures, Lang subverts genre expectations from within, and Ellingboe simply makes a game of history and encourages us to spend some time inhabiting the traumatic lives of the past. All three, and so many more Black artists are haunted. All just tell that same story in different ways. Mark Fisher suggests that these hauntings lead to radical aesthetics, ones that liberate us from a master narrative of white colonial futures (Fisher, 2013, 46). But when Fisher describes hauntology he is describing how Afrofuturist aesthetics challenge dominant white narratives in music. Extending the metaphor to games, Lindsay Grace frets that the ghosts of the past continue to sculpt the discourse around game design (Grace, 2019, 1-2). I concur. Without recognizing how game design is still haunted by themes of colonialism, it is doomed to repeat them. Black radical aesthetics offer a path out of this bind.

Black Game Designers in the Underground

Ellingboe, Lang, and Pondsmith are far from the only Black analog game designers. Although I have singled their work out as particularly inventive Black creators who design against the grain in ways that I feel epitomize Black radical aesthetics, there are many, many, others have been prolific and radical in their work as designers. The publishing conventions of the analog game industry, are, unfortunately still predominantly white. In this section, I look to less conventional publishing spaces—like role-playing game modules,[3] publishing contributions to a larger work, and even self-publishing outside the umbrella of one's own company to locate many other Black analog game designers doing important work.

TK Johnson has been a prolific designer of *Dungeons & Dragons* (2015) supplements for Wizards of the Coast's fan marketplace The Dungeon Master's Guild, which allows designers market their own game supplements after the undergo a review process managed by Wizards. TK's supplements include contributions to *Uncaged II-IV* (2019-2020), a series of adventures that draw on and remix mythology and folklore in order to subvert tropes of female monstrosity; *Book of Seasons: Solstices* (2019), a book of early level adventures meant to

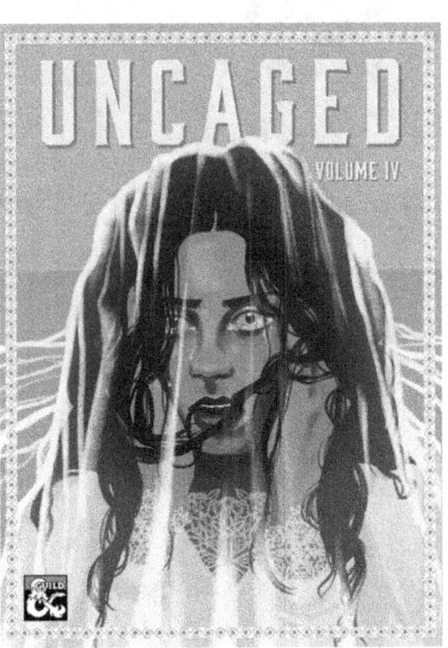

Figure 4 - Cover art of the Uncaged IV collection. Image used for purposes of critique.

supplement uncaged; *Beyond the Basics* (2019), a comedic companion book of creative and unusual encounters; and *Weird*

---

[3] Modules in role-playing games are written adventures intended to supplement the rules of the game itself.

Tales of the British Colonies in the New World (2019) a book of adventures intended to subvert the racist lore of H.P. Lovecraft. Johnson's work is notable as like Lang's-- it generally aims to subvert mythic narratives which have racist and sexist histories.

Jerry D. Grayson runs a small publishing company called Khepera Publishing, and uses it to market the role-playing games that he has authored. Grayson's games use some of the many mechanical engines that he has designed including the modular system *Mythic D6* (2018), and the *Omega System* (2013) which compares twenty-sided dice roles to a standard difficulty scale. The worlds he develops in his games are speculative Black inversions of the worlds developed in typical role-playing games. Indeed, BIPOC characters feature prominently on the cover art of the games Grayson designs, and the lore he builds into his games endeavors to explore culture "in and around Africa" (Grayson, n.d., paragraph 1). His game *GODSEND Agenda* (2001) imagines a future where "man" is minority as they contend with aliens, Atlanteans, transhumans, and an alien blight; *ATLANTIS: The Second Age* (2013) is a sword and sorcery fantasy role-playing game that often prominently features Black people on the covers of its manuals; finally *HELLAS: Worlds of Sun and Stone* (2008) is a is a space opera that imagines Greek mythology in a role-playing setting. Although it is not an explicit part of Grayson's project, he centers Black, brown, and indigenous people in the art and lore of all his games. Subverting the genre conventions, which rarely do the same.

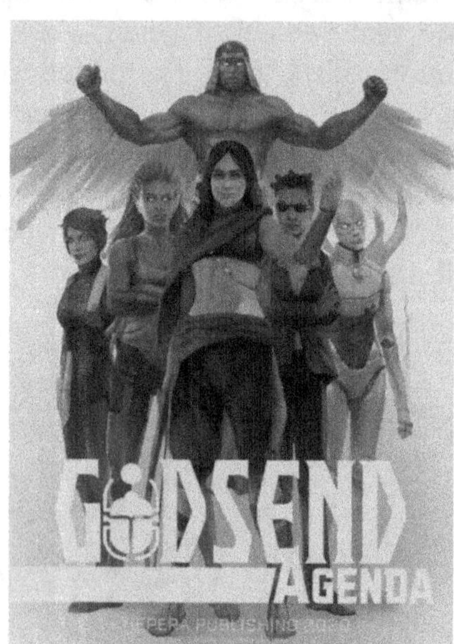

Figure 5 – Cover art for GODSEND: Agenda. Image used for purposes of critique.

Misha Bushyager is another excellent designer in the analog game scene. One of the many games Bushyager has contributed to is *Lovecraftesque* (2017), which won the Italian Gioco Dell'Anno Game of the Year award, and was nominated for a Golden Geek award in 2015. *Lovecraftesque* pulls on many radical conventions in role-playing games by asking players to tell stories without a Dungeon Master spearheading the narrative. This maneuver undermines what bell hooks would term the system of "imperialist white-supremacist capitalist patriarchy" upon which many other role-playing games rely (hooks, n.d., 1). After all, most role-playing games even presume the specter of slavery when the term game or dungeon "Master" is invoked. Bushyager

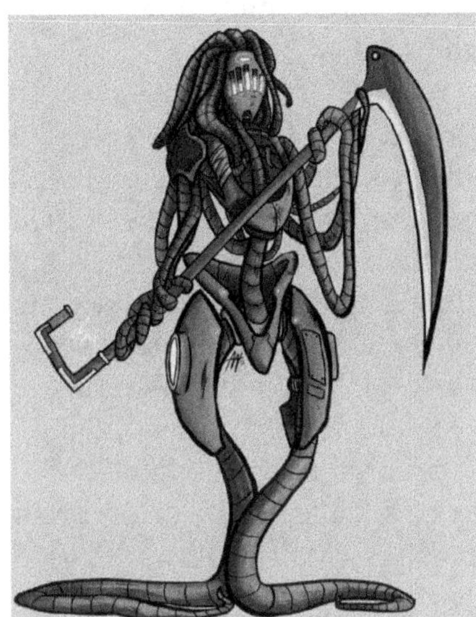

Figure 6 - Character design from the SOurce COde Kickstarter. Image used for purposes of critique.

has also been part of the development of *Orun* (2019), a space opera; *Mispent Youth* (2010), a game about postapocalyptic teenage rebellion; and *Part Time Gods* (2013) a game about the embeddedness of gods, spirituality, and divinity in the mundane activities of everyday life.

One common way that Black designers contribute to the burgeoning analog game scene is by contributing their writing to source books for preexisting games. For example, take Gabrielle Hicks. Hicks excels at bringing lore from the African diaspora into the games he designs. Hicks has contributed to many core books and supplements in the *Pathfinder* (2009) role-playing game engine as well as for the *Dungeons & Dragons* Dungeon Master's Guild including *Darkhold: Secrets of Zhentarim* (2020) and Exploring Ebberon (2020). There are strong elements of Afrofuturism in all of his work. Although he often writes alongside a larger team, he is also the lead designer for *S0urce C0de* (2017) which is a science-fiction tabletop role-playing game that blends fantasy and science fiction. Finally, Hicks has contributed to Tanya DePass's exciting forthcoming role-playing game *Into the Motherlands* (forthcoming).

Stretch goals on Kickstarter, or other crowd funding sites are a different kind of contribution that is also common in the community. Because this work flies under the radar of traditional white owned publishing networks, many Black designers choose to support other members of their community by contributing their time and labor to the stretch goals of the Kickstarters they endorse. Jonaya Kemper is a great example of a Black game designer whose contributions to the community have been made most legible through crowdfunding sites like Kickstarter. Her work has appeared in games like *7th Sea* (2019) a role-playing game that plays with themes of colonialism through swashbuckling and Visigoths vs. Mall Goths (2020) a tabletop role-playing game that addresses outsider identity. Recognizing the role of black analog game designers means recognizing the often understated role of folks like Kemper who develop their skills writing scenarios for systems in the indie scene before eventually penning their own systems and worlds.

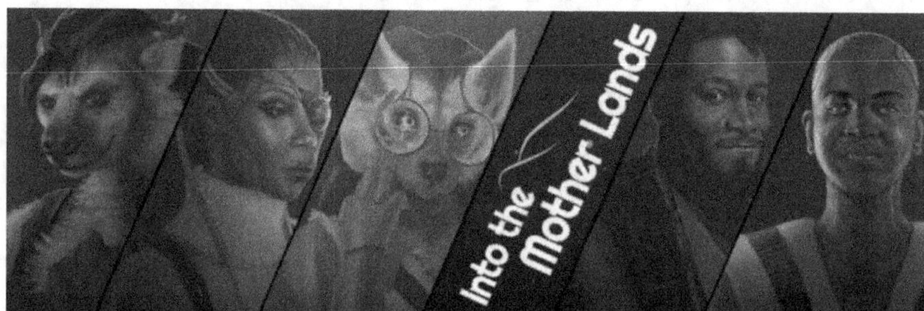

Figure 7 - Banner taken from the Kickstarter for Into the Motherlands. Image use for purposes of critique.

Some members of the community make their mark through activism as well as their work as designers. Tanya DePass is the founder and Director of *I Need Diverse Games*, a non-profit organization devoted to better helping designers from a diverse array of backgrounds better get involved with the creative end of game design. Additionally, she works as a sensitivity consultant on many projects, both analog and digital. An absolute bedrock of the community, she designed the aforementioned *Into the Motherlands*, a role-playing game setting designed only by people of color, and which bills itself with the tagline "A Brighter, Blacker, Future." Like many other role-playing games, the setting is designed within a different proprietary game engine—in this case, the *Cortex Prime* (2016) game engine. In addition to her written contributions to many games like the *Modern Age Companion* (2019), *Pathfinder: Lost Omens World Guide*

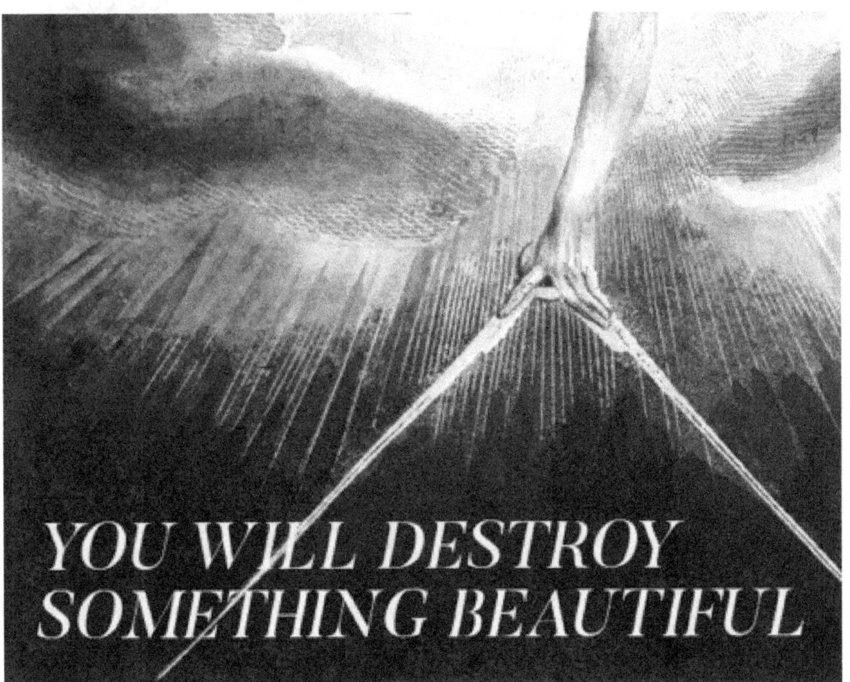

Figure 8 - Cover art for You Will Destroy Something Beautiful. Image used for purposes of critique.

(2019), *Your Best Game Ever* (2019), and *Modern Age: Enemies and Allies* (2020). In sum, DePass's advocacy has been a key part of the game developer industry's push toward diversification between 2010 and 2020, and thus her work as a Black designer—where DePass writes toward a black future—must be acknowledged.

Some other Black game designers work in a truly independent paradigm. For instance Samantha Day sells most of her games on the agile website itch.io—a platform for grassroots game designers to upload their creations to. Although the content on itch.io runs the gamut, Day's games explore the intersection of both queer[4] and Black aesthetics. *Alone in the Void* (n.d.) is a game about isolation, it is a solo role-playing game about exploring space; *Hard Times* (n.d.) tells to story about two feuding gay wrestlers; *You Will Destroy Something Beautiful* (2018) is a short game that encourages players to wrestle with mourning, destruction, and creation; and *Sanctuaire* (n.d.) bills itself as "a belonging outside belonging game of an isolated religious community." Many of Day's games encourage players to question the norms (or absence) of the communities that players imagine themselves within. They are as much about the Blackness as they are about what José Muñoz would term disidentification (Muñoz, 1999, 6). A descriptive term the captures how identifying *against* one's surroundings is often the nexus of subjectivity and self.

Because many Black designers face discrimination in the hobby game industry, they work as entrepreneurs, founding their own imprints to share their ideas with the greater market. For example, Unicorn Motorcycle Games is a tabletop game company that is co-owned by Camdon Wright. Wright's games explore the personal and

----

[4] Bo Ruberg explains some common aesthetics of queer games: "[Queer games] disrupt the status quo, enact resistance, and use play to explore new ways of inhabiting difference." (2020, 3)

intimate aspects of Black identity. He is best known for his game *Madness and Desire* (2020), which simulates a dating show where you are paired with Cthulu. His current project, *One Child's Heart* (2020), makes space for childhood trauma in a play space that is all too frequently dominated by positive accounts of play. Wright's designs epitomize Black radical aesthetics insofar as they encourage players to encounter and explore the subjectivity of the "other" and delve deep into a shared history of trauma that has long been a point of solidarity for Black people since the slave trade.

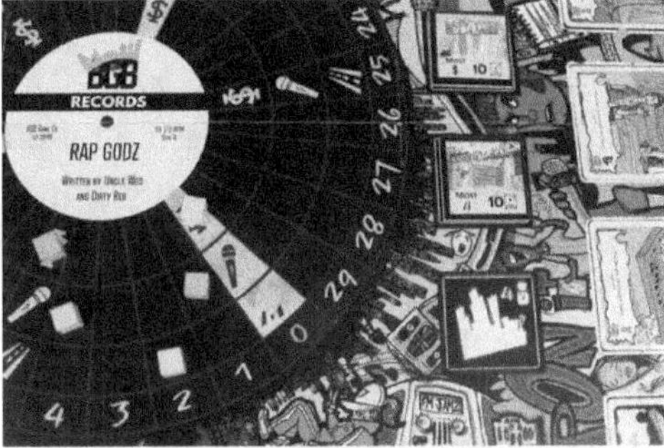

Figure 10 - A photo of Rap Godz taken by Omari Akil. Image used for purposes of critique.

In board games, some of the most provocative Black designs have come from Omari Akil's trailblazing imprint, *Board Game Brothas*. Akil's label puts out board games with a deliberate urban aesthetic, subverting the design aesthetics of the genre overall—which, it must be said, often relies heavily on colonialist tropes that position Black, brown, and indigenous people as secondary, or worse, goods for players to exchange when simulating real world colonial trade. Akil is best known for his game *Rap Godz* (2020), which puts players in the role of an up and coming hip-hop artist looking to

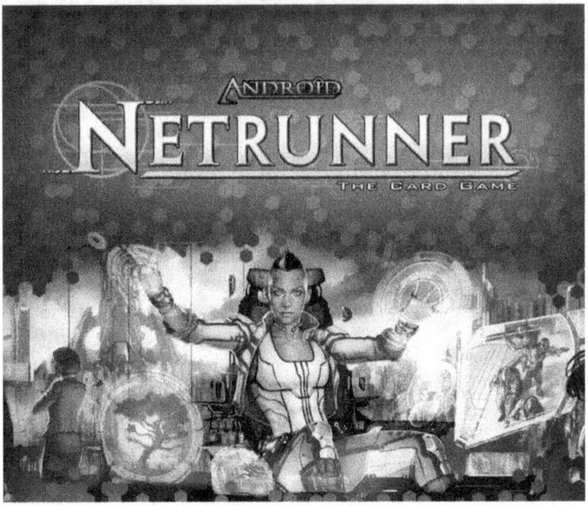

Figure 9 - Cover art for Android: Netrunner. Image by Fantasy Flight Games. CC BY.

51

make it big in the record industry. Akil has also released *Hoop Godz* (2021), which recycles may of the same aesthetic tropes that *Rap Godz* uses, but instead asks players to take the role of basketball players. Again, playing to the interests of Black players in US urban spaces, as opposed to the presumably white audience that many board games are marketed to.

Some designers like Damon Stone, slip under the radar because their name isn't prominently featured on the boxes of the games they design. Stone worked for *Fantasy Flight Games* and was the lead developer for *Netrunner* (2012)—a game designed by *Magic: The Gathering* (1993) designer Richard Garfield, but balanced and developed by Stone in its most recent (and popular) iteration. *Netrunner* was a card game that was based on a good deal of the lore in Pondsmith's *Cyberpunk*, and it's rerelease as part of the *Fantasy Flight Games* lineup in 2012 was celebrated by fans in the community. Under Stone's lead, the game grew to accommodate its thriving tournament scene, as Stone spearheaded the revised rules as well as the development of twelve expansions. While at *Fantasy Flight Games*, Stone was also the developer of several expansions for *Call of Cthulu: The Card Game* (2008) and *Game of Thrones: The Card Game* (2008). Expansions, too, are commonly sold without the designers name on the box.

Designing for Radical Futures

Reviewing the aforementioned examples a reader might be left asking: what does the future of Black analog game design look like? For the future, I hope we see Black designers continue to publish clever, radical, activist, and anti-racist work. Take for example Chris Spivey's *Harlem Unbound* (2017). A game that in many ways captures my enthusiasm for the Black future of game design. *Harlem Unbound* is a role-playing game that takes place in the Harlem Renaissance, and much like the TV Series *Lovecraft Country*, attempts to subvert H.P. Lovecraft's racist world by putting players into the role of Black characters. To the uninitiated, *Harlem Unbound* is a modest package. A complete game based on the *Call of Cthulu* (1981) role-playing game system. As the section prior makes clear, thematic variations built on the rules engine of other role-playing games is a common point of artistic expression in the analog game scene. But rarely do these modifications make the waves that *Harlem Unbound* has. *Harlem Unbound* won three ENnies (analog gaming's grassroots community driven award) and was nominated for a Diana Jones award (an award given to one concept a year by analog gaming's inner circle of luminaries) in 2018. Spivey's work is explicitly anti-racist, and aims to raise a sense of awareness around Black American culture overall.

Harlem Unbound is political in a way that I hope many Black game designers aspire to be. The first pages of the supplement include a scathing takedown of H.P. Lovecraft's work, in a short column entitled, "Lovecraft Was A Racist!" and offer an intimate note by Spivey inviting players to take part in the experience. Spivey acknowledges the critiques that Ellinboe had received—the fear of playing a Black character—and lets players know it's okay to try and make mistakes. The game even begins with a brief history of the Harlem Renaissance—

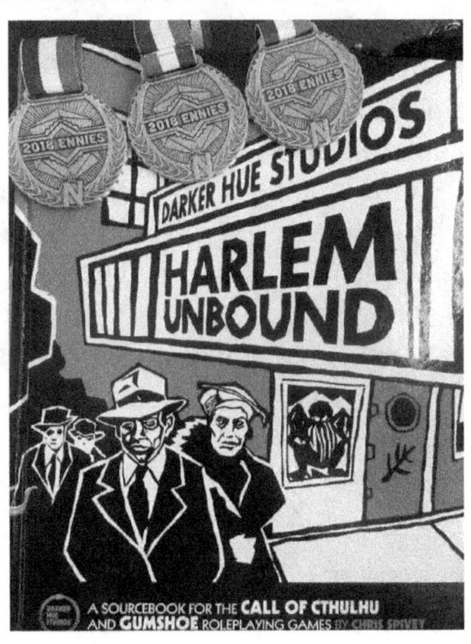

Figure 11 - Cover of the first edition of Harlem Unbound. Image used for purposes of critique.

helping to get readers up to speed with the flourishing Black cultural scene which defined the setting that the game is based upon. The entire manual reads very much as an attempt to normalize Black representation in role-playing games, and to push back against the notoriously white aesthetics that otherwise dominate the genre.

Does *Harlem Unbound* evoke Black Radical aesthetics? I think so. This chapter reads the analog game scene as a space of such white hegemony that any and all Black art that survives, thrives, and excels in this context is itself a radical intervention. A careful reader will have noted that independent publishing companies are a key attribute that unites many Black game designers. This speaks to the greater struggle of Black radical aesthetics in this space, as, well, *it ain't easy.*

Black analog game designers have more trouble finding spaces to publish in an industry that has worked so hard to erase them. This context of oppression, censorship, and exclusion, has itself led to a thriving design scene that has been slowly but surely circling the mainstream of analog games this past thirty years. Fans have been organizing on social media, at cons, and even most importantly, at the gaming table to support Black artists developing analog games. We've come a long way from where the industry started in the homogeneously white early days of the 60s, 70s, and 80s, and there's still much to do in the name of equity. But, as this small, and by definition, inadequately representative sample of Black game designers hopefully shows, Black designers are actively working in the analog game space and their work is profoundly innovative. Their work makes me optimistic for a radical, anti-racist, and inclusive future in game design.

References

1. Carrington, André. 2016. *Speculative Blackness: The Future of Race in Science Fiction*. Minneapolis, MN: University of Minnesota Press.
2. Crooks, Roderic. 2019. Times Thirty: Access, Maintenance, and Justice. *Science, Technology, & Human Values* 44, no. 1. https://doi.org/10.1177/0162243918783053
3. Du Bois, W.E.B. 1994. *The Souls of Black Folk*. Mineola, NY: Dover Publications.
4. Fanon, Frantz. 2008. *Black Skin, White Masks*. London, UK: Pluto Books.
5. Fisher, Mark. 2013. The Metaphysics of Crackle: Afrofuturism and Hauntology. *Dancecult: Journal of Electronic Dance Music Culture* 5, no. 2. https://doi.org/10.12801/1947-5403.2013.05.02.03
6. Grace, Lindsay. 2019. The Unbearable Lightness of Being Game. Proceedings to the 25th International Symposium of Electronic Art (ISEA). Gwangju, South Korea
7. Grayson, Jerry. n.d. About. *Khepera Publishing*. https://kheperapublishing.com/about/
8. hooks, bell. n.d. Understanding Patriarchy. *Imagine No Borders*. https://imaginenoborders.org/pdf/zines/UnderstandingPatriarchy.pdf
9. Jones, Katherine Castiello. 2016. "A Lonely Place": An Interview with Julia Bond Ellingboe. *Analog Game Studies* 3, no. 1. https://analoggamestudies.org/tag/julia-ellingboe/
10. Moten, Fred. 2003. *In the Break: The Aesthetics of the Black Radical Tradition*. Minneapolis, MN: University of Minnesota Press.
11. Muñoz, José Estaban. *Disidentifications: Queers of Color and the Performance of Politics*. Minneapolis, MN: University of Minnesota Press.

12. Muñoz, José Estaban. Feeling Brown, Feeling Down: Latina Affect, the Performativity of Race, and the Depressive Position. *Signs* 31, no. 3, 675-688. https://doi.org/10.1086/499080

13. Robinson, Andy. 2019. Cyberpunk Creator Responds to Criticism. *Video Games Chronicle.* June 19. https://www.videogameschronicle.com/news/cyberpunk-creator-responds-to-2077-criticism-who-do-you-think-you-are/

14. Ruberg, Bonnie. 2020. *The Queer Games Avant-Garde: How LGBTQ Game Makers are Reimagining the Medium of Video Games.* Durham, NC: Duke University Press.

15. Spillers, Hortense. 1987. Mama's Baby, Papa's Maybe: An American Grammar Book. *Diacritics* 17, no. 2. https://doi.org/10.2307/464747

16. Trammell, Aaron. Under Review. *Hobbyists: The Historical Roots of White Geek Masculinity.* Unpublished Manuscript.

17. Torner, Evan, Trammell, Aaron, and Waldron, Emma Leigh. 2014. Reinventing Analog Game Studies. *Analog Game Studies* 1, no. 1. https://analoggamestudies.org/2014/08/reinventing-analog-game-studies/

18. Willis, Robert J. Non-Traditional Casting: A Case Study. *Theatre Topics* 2, no.2. https://doi.org/10.1353/tt.2010.0038

■Black Game Studies

Chapter 4:

An Autobiography of Ehdrigohr

Allen Turner

Overview

"Ehdrigohr: The Roleplaying Game" is an indigenously themed survival horror roleplaying game released in 2013 by Council of Fools LLC. Ehdrigohr is a game of post-cataclysmic, tribal, survival horror. It is a game that explores people coming out of recurring trauma and the social changes they make when they find the opportunity to relax a bit and breathe. It is also a game about fears, anxiety, depression as well as relationships, interdependencies and taking care of each other. Ehdrigohr is also a game that creates a space to explore dogma and tradition by reexamining what continues to serve and what does not. It looks at what traditions are the tools of the trauma space, and how can they unfortunately turn into toxins if we keep them close for too long.

This chapter outlines the author's experience as a designer, reflecting on the design of Ehdrigohr in somewhat autoethnographic terms. The project was successfully funded…. Its aspirations, process, and the experiences that shaped its creation are shared here.

Ehdrigohr has many layers and allows for players to engage as little or as much of it as they want. It focuses on a narrativist, story-driven, play style. It is derived from proprietary systems that are meant to be modified, expanded, and easily accessible for traditional table-top rpg players and newcomers. Play can begin with as little information as a simple idea of what your character is about. Players and game masters can add more details as they go.

◼ Black Game Studies

Prior to releasing Ehdrigohr, this author designer, was a video game designer who worked on multiple releases across different studios. After switching from professional video game development to becoming full time faculty teaching game development at DePaul University's College of Computing and Digital Media, he returned to tabletop work. The tabletop work gave him the breadth and space to write and publish Ehdrigohr.

Ehdrigohr grew out of an ever-transforming ecology of influences and needs. Particularly, there was the need to serve a population that didn't have any cultural predisposition towards mythical ideas like elves, orcs, dwarves, nobles, and other concepts steeped in Eurocentrism while making room for as wide a range of possible players without defaulting to the model of accessibility that colonized and minimized non-Eurocentric perspectives. This exploration of influences and needs is provided through a first-person account of process, iteration, and evolution . The article also explains how Ehdrigohr was informed by Turner's video game development experience and various stages of his life that formed the ecology that nourished the impulse to create. There will also be a breakdown of how moving to video game development helped Turner to create a design process and heuristics as well as how he learned to do community building as part of his design process. These tools allowed for a return to tabletop development and the creation of Ehdrigohr with a much more mindful goal

In the beginning

I am Allen Turner and I'm the designer and publisher of "Ehdrigohr: The Role-playing Game." It's funny to think that many people ask me how I made the switch from doing digital video games to working on Ehdrigohr. It amuses me most often because people think my engagement with games and play experiences began with my tenure making computer and console games. In truth, making video games is when I became more public, displayed more confidence, and grew formally as a game designer. Prior to that I had been creating worlds, writing adventures, and hacking systems on the tabletop side of things, particularly in role-playing games, since my teen years.

Ehdrigohr first manifested in the world way back in 1988. I was a student worker at Columbia College Chicago and I was working the lines for class registrations. Back in those days, registration was a bit of a circus with long lines and tables for sections and categories that you went to register. I was sitting at the table for the computer science department and registering people for their computer classes.

In between the waves of frantic registrants, I was working in a sketchbook making little maps and notes. I had been a long time Advanced Dungeons and Dragons (aka AD&D) (TSR, 1989) fan, and had begun to deep dive into my new love affair with two other role playing games called Rolemaster (Iron Crown Enterprises, 1980) and Talislanta (Bard Games, 1987). I was designing a homebrew campaign world that, in my head, was different from standard AD&D stuff and trying to figure out how to fit it either into Talislanta or Rolemaster. To me they represented opposite ends of the spectrum of role playing games, or rpgs as their more commonly known.

Talislanta was a D20 based system that was D&D distilled down to its bare minimum, in terms of numbers, and then expanded with all sorts of odd creatures and races. Most importantly, for me, it diverged from D&D's "Vancian" style of magic, which was so dubbed because it borrowed from the ideals of Jack Vance's "Dying Earth" novels (Hillman Periodicals, 1950) where wizards had to memorize spells and using them removed them from memory. Talislanta opted for a magic that had a simple set of spells with graduated power which were cast off the cuff with a skill roll. My brain read the various peoples in Talislanta as a cultured world as opposed to a D&D world which just had what felt like arbitrary races and monsters who were just part of a catalog of tropes, and magic that felt mechanical to me and seemed to lack that freeform wonder.

Rolemaster, on the other hand, was something of a build it yourself space. It was very skill and choice based as you built characters, and its chart-based resolution system was very, very cinematic. It was the only game that let you have that kind of fight where you were up against all odds, bleeding out fighting with your good arm and then post-victory your character might take a few steps back, sit on a rock and die satisfied you made a difference. That's how it read to me at least. This was important because it very much represented the kind of cinematic, epic action type of stories I wanted to tell.

So, the nascent version of Ehdrigohr existed in that space as a few hand drawn world maps and lots of character creation and monster notes. It was a bit system agnostic, and I would spend numerous years trying to find the right system for it. When I started doing forensic animation work, I shelved Ehdrigohr. This was mostly because, at that time, Ehdrigohr was a soulless thing, and I wasn't sure what to do with it.
Imagining with youth

In 1990 I became a prevention worker for American Indian Health Services (AIHS) in Chicago. I was basically doing youth work and social work. I had this mob of kids I was taking care of day in and day out, and they were like my little brothers and sisters. Some were actually not that much younger than I was. I had no formal training around how to manage these youth, but I did have a lot of imagination. We didn't have much in the way of access to physical spaces where we could easily bring everyone together for activities and play. So, I did the next best thing, in my opinion, by introducing them to tabletop rpgs.

Every Sunday for around 2 years we'd meet in the AIHS afterschool room and play roleplaying games from about 10am to 5pm. It was like church for them and me. Play church. It did take a little bit of doing to find something that clicked with the majority of them. It was coming up against the cultural limitations of most tabletop rpgs at the time that inspired me to dust off Ehdrigohr and see if I could tweak it to make it accessible to them. The kids liked AD&D though they didn't like any of the settings. That struggle caused me to go back to trying to stuff Ehdrigohr into the Advanced Dungeons and Dragons ruleset.

My kids were multi-ethnic, multicultural, and multi-tribal. These kids experienced transient lives as their families moved about, going back and forth from the city to their reservations. They knew a lot about their own tribal cultures but had no connection to things like elves and dwarves. This was the watershed moment that caused Ehdrigohr to be a primarily BIPOC space. I worked much better to dispense with the idea of races and to embrace a multicultural human-centric world.

I actually played two games with them, to varying degrees. The first was Ehdrigohr under AD&D rules. The second was another setting I created called the "Tales of the White Peacock Society" which was a superhero setting that used the original "Marvel Super Heroes Roleplaying Game" (TSR, 1984) as its ruleset. While Ehdrigohr was more standard fantasy, in the White Peacock Society the kids belonged to a bird themed order that worked to protect the world against monsters and villains that arose from bad ideas and bad thoughts that manifested in the world. They loved that game, and it got the lion's share of playtime. The structure of belonging to this magical medicine society had a great pull and provided an easily accessible on-ramp for what they were expected to be doing.

My job at AIHS came to an end and I transitioned to being the guy to run the youth program at the American Indian Center (AIC). In this space I began to amalgamate some of the better ideas between the superhero game and the D&D game and Ehdrigohr began to take on a life. When the AIC shuttered its doors for a while I went to work at Native American Educational Studies College (NAES College) where I ran the Family Education Model for Academic Excellence. It was still community driven and I was interfacing with families and kids and their interactions with Chicago Public Schools. I also ran General Education Development (GED) classes for youth and adults who had not graduated highschool and needed to take the GED test to get their diploma, as well as taught storytelling workshops. Here was where I had the resources and support to start considering this idea of games as a parable for other experiences. I had the idea but not the words to break it down yet. What I did do was start rewriting Ehdrigohr as a fully Indigenously themed world and the setting began to come alive.

Eventually funding for that program came to an end as my first child was born. I was left in between jobs so I opted to be a stay-at-home dad for a time. Ehdrigohr got worked on in bits and pieces during that time and it slowly came together as its own unique thing, but it still wasn't quite right. I thought I had something that I might be able to publish, so I kept poking at it without really understanding what needed to change. This was hard because I was struggling with the big picture and I didn't know what was the main idea that I was trying to get to. This meant I didn't really know what I was trying to say or express through this game, so I often got stuck.

Resources and roadblocks

I had actually almost released Ehdrigohr to the world back in 1996 when I was at home, between jobs, taking care of my first child. I never got to a point where I was really happy with it though. There were some interesting nuggets for sure, but It was still really just more of the same but with some Native trappings to it. I eventually stepped back from the project, and shelved it, when I got hired at Bungie Software in 1997.

Ehdrigohr's biggest nugget back then was that it was really just an AD&D world with some indigenous and POC themes. Those themes were being heavily affected by the urge to make something that focused around Native and indigenous cultures and less around traditional Euro-fantasy. I was finding that those themes didn't mesh so well with the play structures of the game which was Advanced

Dungeons and Dragons, Second Edition (TSR, 1989). I wasn't really approaching it from an experiential point of view or with an overarching narrative. It was more just identifying archetypes I wanted to see and trying to build them out of the rules as written.

What I was bumping heads against is that the rules of AD&D were culturally built to model ideals and archetypes from capitalist, colonialist culture and would always minimize the impact of other cultural expressions or convert them to a colonial model which repeatedly would leave me frustrated with the results. Success in that game was defined by gold piece values and vertical power structures. I wasn't aware of that at the time. I was only aware that the results always felt empty. It left me feeling like I was missing the mark somehow, somewhere.

After considerable frustration with it, I eventually shelved the project again. It was around that time that I got involved with video game design. Digging into the world of video game design was the best choice I could have made as a young designer because it forced me to reevaluate my tools and my processes. Video games have inherent limitations and awesome opportunities to be navigated that are different from what one is used to when coming from table-top design.

Let me take a moment to break that down a bit.

In table-top, imagination is the rendering engine. In that space rules and procedures are your mechanisms for driving narrative forward. While you have varying types of static tokens, the narrative plays out in an overlapping imaginal space that exists in the minds of the players.

To me, this makes creating narrative spaces considerably easier on tabletop. It also makes it easy to get lost in the space of making rules and procedures in an effort to model events. We see this a lot in the more math drive, often refereed to as "more crunchy," table-top roleplaying games.

What those events look like in each player's head may be slightly different, but the stimulus and results are agreed upon and mediated by the game's structure. The major creative economic costs lie in the effort to make physical materials with which to play, and possibly paying artists and writers if you are collaborating in a team of some sort.

In video games, it's different because the focus is very much on the limits of the rendering engine and hardware. There are typically no physical materials to consider but there are the costs of deployment resources (renderer, memory, bandwidth, etc.) to consider and those limitations are typically the driver of design . Every modeled event requires code to allow it to happen and art, sound, and animation to punctuate and provide feedback. One can't rely on the player(s) providing, and interpreting, all of that themselves. Video games require the designer to create and hold the space much more directly and a certain amount of scaffolding of the social space and social contracts in a way that I think is often taken for granted in the tabletop space.

Lastly there is the idea that video games are temporary in a way that tabletop is not. Video games exist in a temporal bubble bounded by the technology they are delivered on. As that tech continues to change, the video game eventually becomes unplayable unless someone is doing the work to keep it updated alongside the technology.

I have, for instance, an old copy of the boardgame Titan (Avalon Hill, 1982) that I dust off from time to time to play with friends, and that copy is 39 years old. It's considerably harder to do that with my old copy of Magic Carpet (Bullfrog, 1994) unless I go out of my way to set up my system with an emulator.

This temporality becomes an even bigger issue when we start talking about making a culturally aware video game. Since the technology platforms are typically owned by third parties, the struggle to archive can get caught in a gatekeeping space as the capacity to archive might not always be in the hands of the creator of the work or the people that the work is intended for. Someone has to have sufficient funds and access to the technology of the platform to keep the video game accessible and viable. If the platform owner ceases support for the platform or the creators pass on and access to the original code is no longer available, the work may fade into obscurity and be unrecoverable other than articles, videos, and screenshots of it. With a table-top game the worst that can happen is that it falls out of publication or circulation. In this case there still artifacts that can be resold or redistributed second hand and they remain playable in their analog form.

So, as I found out, going into the video game world, the list of differences is huge. Even greater is the considerable amount of technical knowhow that one must bring to bear to create one. This resulted, for me, in a little bit of culture shock and effort shock around how much work, and how restrictive it is to make a video game. This was important because it made me stop and reconsider what I thought I knew and the hows and whys behind every decision to include something in a video game. While one must do this in the tabletop space, for differing reasons, I wasn't doing that back then. I was still somewhere in the space between consumer and creator. Video game work was the impulse that made me change that and wake up to the processes and much more mindful creation.

It was the experience of struggling in that liminal space between consumer and creator and connecting to the mindful processes inbetween that made me into a designer.

Days of Bungie past

So, back to the shelving of Ehdrigohr and the video game switch. I shelved Ehdrigohr and joined Bungie Inc in 1997, in Chicago, as part of their production and support staff. That was the beginning of a whole new world for me. Myth: The Fallen Lords (Bungie 1997) had been released and Marathon II Durandal port for PC (Bungie 1996) was relatively new to the market as well.

My role was tech support but, since we were a small company and everything was inhouse, I had to interface directly with the design teams to work through issues. Sometimes it meant that I even got to help design solutions and then put them through testing before they went out to the public.

Interfacing with the public taught me a lot about how wildly wrong things can go when the public has ideas about how a mechanic should be used or what they mean that are considerably different from those of the designers. There was so much hand holding that had to happen to set expectations, and so much feedback that was needed to keep players guided. It's common sense now, especially considering how much academic space has grown up around games recently, but back then it was really eye-opening.

As we moved into the development of Myth II (Bungie, 1998), I developed a closer relationship with the design team. This afforded me an opportunity to watch and participate in the process of developing from the ground up. Bungie was very driven by strong narratives, and everything was homegrown. This was before the time of rampant use of 3rd party engines. Time was money so what we chose to add and what we chose to not add was hugely important. Every decision had profound time and money costs. We had lists of "Things that rock" that spoke to story elements and cinematic moments that we wanted the player to be able to experience. Identifying those narrative hooks allowed for foundations to build play structures around. In addition, we had a community that we had to manage and keep appetized while we figured out the next chapter. A lot of my job was in the latter. There was also the intent of opening up the game by releasing the dev tools, so a chunk of my job became learning the tools and creating documentation for the community.

The part that was most informative for me was the playtesting. Playing every little nook and cranny of the game, ad nauseum, helped me to better understand the constraints the dev team was working under and the struggles they had to maintain narrative. There were opportunities to directly influence and help redesign some of the game levels because in test, they revealed many places where they broke functionally or felt narratively disjointed. There were many things the development team wanted to add but time and other resources prevented.

That playtesting back and forth was a huge piece of my personal research into how to do this kind of development. It was eye opening to see a problem, think there was an easy fix by doing some cool thing that I could see in my head, but then to converse with programmers and artists about why a thing couldn't be done or why it could or should, began to shape my worldview into a combination of the interplay of finite resources and creating experiences. This was a lens that I previously had not used to approach any game or creation of play. It became an essential lens because it helped me to focus on the essential bits when I got back to working on it.

The other part of this that was an influential learning experience was the process of keeping fans appetized and engaged for a thing that did not exist yet. With Myth II, in particular, it was also trying to engage new audiences. So that meant jumping around lots of different forums and news groups and engaging people in conversations about the game or subjects related to the game. It was less about hard sales or up sales and more about relationship building and managing expectations. In a time before "Games as a service" was a thing, we were of a mindset that this was less about launching a product and more about building a community. Other studios that I would subsequently come to work for did considerably less of this as they were typically controlled by a publisher who had a marketing team which would work at building appetite for the product, but they were far more removed from the project than the dev' and support teams we had at Bungie.

When I returned to working on Ehdrigohr, I took a similar approach. Connecting with the community the way we did at Bungie became a design pillar for me. I made a point to maneuver around in various online spaces and talk about the projects, solicit feedback for various ideas, and drop bits of lore and concepts for people to mull over. The secondary benefit to doing this was that rather than appearing to arrive out of nowhere, if you searched the name of the game or my name, then you'd get a ton of hits that gave the image of history and conversations that presaged the arrival of the game. It showed that I was a real person and that there was a lot of persevering passion behind this project.

Robots and Rampages

I took my first actual design position in the autumn of 2003 with Day1Studios (which has since t been shuttered and absorbed into World of Tanks). Day1Studios was a very different creative environment from the former Bungie. I was working on the single player campaign for the game "MechAssault" (Microsoft Game Studios, 2002) which would also be a launch title for the first incarnation of Xbox Live.

This was different, experientially, from my production team and support work at Bungie. It was much more ground up creation and I had the opportunity to directly affect the narrative. There were place holders for missions and their planetary environments, but each designer had to flesh out the particulars. The project had been struggling for some definition for a while and so it was in the hands of the newly hired game designers to help shape it into something solid. It was like being the director of my own mini-movie production. Unlike the original Intellectual property (IP) we worked on at Bungie, Day1Studios was working with third party legacy IP which brought a number of constraints with that creative process.

At Day1 there was much more focus on the gameplay, product, and brand and less focus on community building. We didn't actually have a story when I came on. The story came in the latter portion of development once we had enough game to decide what kind of interactions we could wrap narrative around to make a good tale.

This was an interesting learning space because the focus was ultimately staying as true to the brand while also creating a new experience. We weren't really asking much about which characters did what and what the deep overarching storyline was. We were instead asking what seemed fun and plausible to do within the context of the legacy of this setting.

This was a struggle for me at first. It was the designing within the boxed-in space of the brand that was the problem. There was a lot of legacy information from previous incarnations of Battletech (FASA, 1984) which one had to consume to be able to create in this setting. For me this was tough, as I had been used to being able to just make whatever sparked my fancy. Everything I had done up until that point had been open ended and there was always room to add something new. In this creative space that wasn't the case. We could tell new stories, but we couldn't contradict existing stories and we couldn't do anything that changed the setting. Everything had to work within the conceits of the Battletech universe, while at the same time leaning in on the things that were fun about our gameplay which was much more action packed than previous video game versions of Battletech experiences. Those had all been slower moving and methodical tactical interactions. We had to stay true to the experience of the brand and stay true to the experience of the game's core play conceits.

What came out of this for me was lots of process tools and that there is a type of fun to be had in designing in restricted spaces. It really helped to identify some hard boundaries. Those things were integral to shaping the overall experiences. While my previous attempts at creating games from branded settings had typically seen me doing my best to remake, break, or subvert the setting, I had never really sat down to identify the experience a setting offers, and the joys derived by its players. It was easy to subvert and break it because I was working towards my own particular likes, but I was not necessarily actually creating a new experience. Having to stay in the box with MechAssault really helped me to see the fun and creative power of building within limits to enhance the default experience of a brand without having to break it to do so.

A Wide Load of Lenses

Hot on the heels of my successes with MechAssault, I reconnected with a number of old friends from Bungie and we started Wideload Games. The intent with Wideload had been to create comedic games. The Wideload flavor was this off the wall, almost Mad Magazine style of humor. It's a humor that fell into the same kind of narrative space occupied by studios like Shiny and Black Box games. This was a fun change of pace from making your standard epic action games with a militarized bent to them. It also had the problem, for me, that this particular humor style was very much a culturally White cis-gendered male privileged kind of humor. It relied often on tropes that were a bit outside of my experience range, so I had to learn what that funny looked like.

I pitched a lot of games but many of my attempts at new IP fell flat because they relied on tropes that were more from Black, People of Color (POC), and other such experiences. I think this was when I was switching my mindset to think about games that might have a message in them. I like the idea of humor as a medium for the message because it could make the process of receiving the message felt non-threatening. Again, this was a tough sell as the Wideload flavor of humor was big on shock value and in your face gags that bordered on puerile (lots of fart, dick, and scat jokes, lots of slapstick) but they were resistant to humor that was challenging or thought-provoking in a social conscious kind of way. They didn't want to open the "politics" can of worms. So much of what I pitched (which were typically POC and identity-centered in their humor) were written off as being Blacksploitation (and some of them certainly did fall into that category, to be fair). We did revisit the ideas several times, coming back because people liked the idea of the games but danced around situations that would leave us with a POC protagonist and open us up to hard conversations that our publishers were also not ready to have.

As a matter of "code switching", acclimating to the environment, survival and connecting with my colleagues, I slowly learned to create, in play, the style of humor that pervaded the office. Though I can't help wondering what games like Stubbs the Zombie would have been like if we had leaned into zombies as a metaphor for the civil rights movement as had been my original want. Over time, my need to make things that spoke from more marginalized voices would grow. I realized that these jobs weren't a space yet for me to tell my stories. I was still telling colonizer stories. They were fun, but they didn't really speak to me.

Stubbs the Zombie was my first, truly from the ground up, development experience. Moreso than MechAssault because I was part of the high-level concepting before we even got to the building of the game. It was nice because it was a return to creating in a space unbounded by a previous legacy brand. It was fun to think about interesting zombie tropes and decide which one we were going to support and which we were going to subvert. There was a lot learned about setting appetite for a new idea and figuring out how to sell it to a publisher.

Once we were done with Stubbs, I was feeling really good about my skills as a game designer and play creator. I had a knack for finding bits of play that really punctuated particular experiences that we wanted the player to have. I was still doing it all on instinct though. I didn't have a plan or a process. I just basically threw tons of ideas at the wall until something stuck.

After Stubbs, I started adjunct teaching nights at DePaul University. I was teaching game design classes. This forced me to start thinking about how to explain to people how to do what I do. It also meant I began reading work by the likes of Katie Salens, Jane McGonigal, Jessie Schell, and Tracy Fullerton. Each of these creators introduced me to lots of ways to break down ideas. "Rules of Play" (MIT Press, 2003) and "Game Design Workshop" (Kaufman, 2008) did so much to help me contextualize structures, mechanisms and ideas. "Reality is Broken" (Penguin, 011) really caused me to take a step back and think about the process of game design in an ecology where it can affect the general wellbeing of the people that engage with it. It was, however, discovering "Art of Game Design: A Book of Lenses" (Kaufman, 2008) which was my big aha moment.

The idea of breaking a game experience down and looking at it through a set of experience lenses just completely clicked in my head. It was what I had been doing, I just hadn't had those words to describe it. When I came across that structure, I totally saw my process as being akin to the contraption that an Optometrist uses to check your vision. They ask which is better and flip between lenses and you provide feedback on what is working and what is not. They retire the lenses that don't work and double down on the ones that do. It's a process of continuous refinement.

I put this process to work, in earnest, on the game Disney's Guilty Party. It was a mystery game on the Wii designed to celebrate the tropes of whodunit mystery novels, the treasure hunts of games like "Where in the World is Carmen San Diego" (Broderbund, 1985), the silliness of mini-game driven games like "Warioware Smooth Moves" (Nintendo, 2007), and to be family friendly and accessible.

Using the process of lenses, I was able to break down the big ideas of whodunnit fiction, and identify play tropes and experiences that I thought were integral to the genre (as we knew it and as we were building it) and then use those lenses to closely examine all the bits of play and minigames we were making for the game. This led to some wildly successful results. It allowed me to come up with upwards of 60 minigames, each with 3 difficulty levels, and a small subset which were multiplayer and allowed for different numbers of players while maintaining 3 difficulty levels. The difficulty adjustments were sufficient to make each difficulty a newish singular game. This ended up with over 150 minigames and a multiplayer player vs player board game mode that allowed for always interesting play. Other members of the team devised the rules for how mysteries worked, which allowed us to create a game with seemingly unending numbers of mysteries to sort out which were randomly generated.

I carried the momentum of creation from this project into our next project which was working on Marvel games and uniting a Marvel gaming universe. We put forth many awesome game ideas, some of which were very engaging and complex, but they ran afoul of changing business models. We did manage to get out Marvel Infinity: Hulk and I designed Marvel XP to be a unified meta-space that told a story that unified all of the different Marvel games in production as Marvel/Disney. Unfortunately, as I said before, the game business model at Disney was changing to a Free-to-Play model and that wound up squashing the other Marvel games that were in production.

As I had been working on these games, I was really connecting to the idea of defining an overall experience early on and then doing everything I could to create play that became little rituals that connected the player to that experience. I was in love with the process and was amazed at how intimately it connected me to the games I was making. Everything I was making though, had these legacy brand boundaries, which limited how far I could go to tell a tale and what I could do with characters or what power I could give to the player. I really found myself wanting to tell deeper, more meaningful, and more personal stories and I was not able to do that in my creative space at Wideload/Disney. We had moved to a free-to-play game structure and a general business and monetizing driven design model and away from an experience driven design model.

So, I quit.

Return to Ehdrigohr, A new beginning

I started teaching fulltime and that gave me the space to look at where I'd been and what I had been doing. I really wanted to make something of my own, so I found myself digging up the old bits of Ehdrigohr that I hadn't touched in years.

When I looked at the project, as it was, through my new lenses, I realized it was a mess. It was trying way too hard to be accessible to a mainstream audience and included lots of arbitrary junk that really wasn't part of the story I wanted to tell.

What I was working on didn't have any real boundaries or a branded experience to contain it. Everything was arbitrary and there because I'd seen it in other games. It was a collection of curated ideas, but it didn't have its own identity. It needed that to stand out and to help me define what was interesting about playing in this space.

So, I sat down to make a list of my lenses for Ehdrigohr. I wanted the following things:

- A game that looked at the world through an indigenous eye.
- A game that was horror, but not mired down in depravity and nihilism.
- A dark world in a space of recovery, where hope and moving from surviving to thriving were the goals.
- An experience that acknowledged the struggles with identity and being seen that affects so many of us and feeds depression.
- An indigenous space that was non-colonized.

●A human centric world that had such variations between the cultures that they all seemed widely magical.
●An experience that allowed for a wider range of gender expectations and roles, and different family patterns.
●Family had to have meaning and community was part of your wealth.
●I wanted something that focused around telling good stories of overcoming and perseverance.

I had switched from seeing the indigeneity in my world through a lens of cultural performance and regalia, to a lens of interaction and worldview. Ehdrigohr needed to allow for a wide range of peoples but always keep an indigenous perspective. To me this was the same as how D&D allowed for so many different worlds, but always came about them from a Euro-colonizer perspective. That perspective affected what was seen to be effective or powerful. It affected what was seen to be elegant and what was seen to be broken.

Looking at the Ehdrigohr that I had through these lenses, led to some drastic changes. I wound up throwing away easily 90% of what I had written before. This was mostly because I recognized that much of what was written was focused around more "traditional" rulesets and expectations for fantasy fiction.

Looking through a lens of "no colonization" was the first pass and it resulted in the removal of large Euro-feeling kingdoms and a focusing in on large tribal groups typically overseen by a democratic council of some such. Every culture was rewritten in a way that made their survival process evident and how they connected to their ecology and each other. There was also the removal of "evil races" and focusing on culture and institutional choices. This meant that all the cultures had some problematic things going on and teetered at the edge of being sustainable and non-sustainable.

In addition to "no colonization" I had developed a lens that was about the "emotional turmoil of survival" and its toll. Being an abuse survivor myself (and finding myself often at odds with the old wounds and stories in my head) I began to wonder about the experience of survival.

I realized that survival was not really about beating down monsters, though that was certainly a fun part of it. Survival needed to be about the emotional labor of the aftermath. I was concerned about what happens with all the trauma experienced by people who are in a survival state all the time. Looking around me at the generations of Black and Indigenous people in my life, I realized it was more than the simple getting stronger model that many game structures adhere to. When I looked closer at my own survival story, I found an answer that I could work into the lore of the world and into the experience of the rules and play.

At the time I was working through some identity issues centered around belonging, as well as some depression that came out of some family struggles. I could see how profound an infection a little bit of depression could be to a community and I wanted to make that a tangible influence in the game. I could see an epidemic of depression around me, and I could see how so much of the depression was coming from intergenerational trauma. These old stories of survival and pain were slowly wrapping people in this invisible prison of sorrow.

That brought about the introduction of Sorrow and the Shivers as game characters. Shivers weren't an evil race; they were a voracious deconstructor. They were part of the depression metaphor, these anxieties that come clawing at you in the dark spaces. They whittle away at what nourishes you.

Sorrow, itself, was the ultimate depression metaphor. It was a catalyst for the decomposition of one's emotional wellbeing so much that the infected would just become a stain in the world whose very sight would instigate a new infection of sorrow in the viewer. Because I was building a game where your story was super important, Sorrow became a mechanic for losing faith in your story and not being able to be self-sustaining or lean on one's successes.

One simply stopped believing in themselves so much, that they ceased to be.

Speaking of the importance of story, that also became a lens I wanted to push the game narrative through. So many of the games I had been trying to use to build Ehdrigohr were mired in modeling the mechanics of battle and balanced themselves around ensuring that a character was never too powerful or too weak in an individual skirmish session. As much as I wanted awesome battles, I didn't want the game to just be about the mechanical particulars of battle. I wanted something that focused on a mythic space that brought all participants further into the telling of a great story that had mythic qualities.

Looking through this storytelling lens led me to scrap the previous game systems I'd used, and even to scrap my attempts at my own game system because it was derivative of the problematic systems and inherited their problems. I wanted something more freeform but not so freeform as to paralyze players with options. I wanted the core ruleset to help set appetite and expectations in a way that made sense. In D&D for instance the sense of the character belongs to the rules of D&D that creates its own genre of fantasy with certain expectations on magic and hefty cosmological ideals. When one created a character, the player worked to make a character from the allowable rule bits and offerings and you can't stray too far from that. If you made a wizard or a monk, you did it the D&D way and that structure defines what you are allowed to do. The story really has no bearing here other than to give you some extra proficiencies, feats, or stat benefits. Everything is defined by tactical restrictions and allowances. I wanted the character creation to follow the conceits of the world and not necessarily be strictly defined by the rules. I wanted the fantasy to be the thing that was being modeled and the story of it to have an impact in play regularly.

This led me to the Fate Core system (Evil Hat, 2013) which I felt was a decent marriage between the more crunchy and mathy systems and the more esoteric story only systems. What I liked about it was that it did a lot to make the story an active resource in the play and manipulating that story resource became the focus. This was important because it meant that backstory wasn't arbitrary. It also meant backstory wasn't purely mechanical in that sense that it gave your character extra points or resources to spend and then get forgotten as happens in so many games that focus on a merit and flaw process for creating characters.

Using Fate meant that, through the idea of aspects, I could create an expectation for the player of a story tying you to the world and to your character. No need for alignments because who you are is already in your aspects. No need for endless catalogs of items and weapons because the important stuff is already part of your aspects. The aspects gave me something to tie hope and, more importantly, Sorrow to.

By asking the player to do all of this backstory work, we ensure that every game has a built-in prehistory that gives meaning to the setting for the players and gave meaning to the character for the player. That meaning would eventually be used to pull them through a narrative. It also set the stage for deciding what a character was capable of and would be a powerful resource for the player to use to affect the narrative of a given scene or skirmish. It gave them a story of self-belief which could be slowly ablated as Sorrow set in. The social ties developed in the story of character creation would be necessary for building ritual and healing to cleanse a character of Sorrow later in the game. Anyone with too much Sorrow literally lost sight of their own story and the value of themselves in the bigger narrative. They withered into a black stain of nothingness which would be Sorrow inducing for others.

Once I had these big ideas sorted, they made room for all of the other lenses. Much like assembling the outer perimeter of a puzzle first, I could suddenly see where and how all of the other pieces would fit. Magical ideals and cosmologies were easy to build in a way that supported the core themes of narrative, related bits and interdependence. It made it easy to scaffold for different types of fantasy ideas without putting down hard templates. People could start playing with very little information or after having sat down to read the whole book and system.

When all was said and done, I had a world that was wounded, had survived multiple terrible ordeals, and was trying to right itself. It was a survival horror story about hope and community and not about how rotten or twisted your characters could get. It was a place where creation was still happening. Though it was inspired by so many different types of narratives and experiences I was exposed to in my life, it isn't a strict model of any one of them.

Different people will get different things out of the final result. Those who want a statistical modeling experience of fighting with spears in the prairie heat aren't going to find that in this game. Those who want to tell an interesting and mythic story will certainly find the tools to do that. Characters in Ehdrigohr are certainly heartier than they are in your average fantasy game. They're harder to kill and die spectacularly. Every death is an opportunity for hope or debilitating sorrow. In that space battles become a necessity and not necessarily the point. What happens after is where the more interesting part of the tale lies.

I'm very proud of the game and setting that finally manifested as Ehdrigohr, despite any imperfections it may have as my first big individual work. It actively makes room for so many different types of people and their ideas. I've had people come to me in conventions and tell me of profound and heartfelt moments of feeling seen they'd had when they sat down to explore the work. If I had published what I had when I was younger it would have been just another derivative, dismissible fantasy setting with tinges of Eurocentricity. Stepping away from Ehdrigohr for years and engaging and enduring the processes of mindful game design I was exposed to across my multiple stops in my journey caused the basic idea to marinate. It made the difference between something basic and something that was filled with life and experience. I developed a great understanding of cultivating a culture around a game, designing within boundaries, appreciating the value of setting, and creating mechanics and narrative that keep the player immersed in an experience and punctuate the big metaphors of the narrative. I am a better designer for having done all of these things.

References

1. "Advanced Dungeons and Dragons,2nd Edition Player's Handbook." Lake Geneva, WI, USA: (New York): TSR; Distributed to the book trade by Random House, 1989
2. "Magic Carpet." Electronic Arts, Bullfrog, 1994
3. "Marathon II: Durandal." Bungie Inc., 1995 (Mac), 1996 (PC)
4. "MechAssault." Microsoft Game Studios/Day1 Studios, 2002
5. "Myth II: Soulblighter." Bungie Inc., 1998
6. "Myth: The Fallen Lords." Bungie Inc., 1997
7. "Warioware Smooth Moves." Nintendo of America, 2007
8. "Where in the World is Carmen San Diego?" Broderbund, The Learning company, 1985
9. Donohue, Rob and Hicks, Fred. "Fate: Core system" Evil Hat productions, 2013
10. Fenlon, Peter C, and Ruemmler, John David. "Rolemaster", 1st edition. Iron Crown Enterprises 1982
11. Fullerton, Tracy, Christopher Swain, and Steven Hoffman. 2008. Game design workshop: a playcentric approach to creating innovative games. Amsterdam: Elsevier Morgan Kaufmann.
12. Grub, Jeff. "Marvel Super Heroes Roleplaying Game." TSR,1984
13. McAllister, Jason and Trampier, David. "Titan." Avalon Hill, Valley Games, 1980
14. *McGonigal, Jane. Reality Is Broken : Why Games Make Us Better and How They Can Change the World. London :Jonathan Cape, Penguin 2011.*

15. *Schell, Jesse. The Art of Game Design : a Book of Lenses. Amsterdam ; Boston :Elsevier/Morgan Kaufmann, 2008*

16. Sechi, Stephen Michael. "The Talislantan Handbook." Bard Games, 1987

17. Tekinbaş, Katie Salen, and Eric Zimmerman. 2003. Rules of play: game design fundamentals. Cambridge, Mass: MIT Press.

18. Turner, Allen, 2013. "Ehdrigohr: The Roleplaying Game." DriveThruRpg POD.

19. Vance, Jack. "The Dying Earth." Hillman Periodicals. 1950

20. Weisman, Jordan and Babcock III, L. Ross, and Lewis, Sam. "Battletech." FASA Corporation,1984

Chapter 5:

On Procedural Rhetoric and Designing Black Like Me

Lindsay Grace

Overview

This chapter describes the theory and implementation of a 2-tiered procedural rhetoric game. The game, Black Like Me, employs critical design to encourage players toward situational analysis instead of mere attribute matching. Players are presented with a color matching game at the surface, but the game is designed to reward players for holistically evaluating a scene and subverting the explicitly suggested game rules. The game is designed to train players toward perceiving ambiguity and employing alternative play strategies. This chapter is a reprint of the 2013 Foundations of Digital Games paper on the design of digital games to provide context for the design practice. It is provided here to augment the understanding of digital design practices by Black game makers and to balance the largely analog focus of the prior chapters.

Critical Gameplay

The Critical Gameplay project was a decade-long project to create and embed critical design games. The games have been exhibited at a variety of academic showcases, creative exhibits and related events in through Europe, the Americas and Asia. It is an effort to raise awareness around game design assumptions that permeate traditional play (Grace, 2014) and a case study in the foundation from which the authors social impact design focuses (Grace, 2019). Since 2009 the games have been displayed at more than 50 venues.

On Procedural Rhetoric: Designing Black Like Me ■

Game designers are often reluctant to embrace alternative play within the systems they create. In reality some of the most successful play experiences are about designers merely providing a set of toys through which players can explore concepts. This is true of megahits like Minecraft and World of Warcraft to construction set franchises like Civilization, The Sims and Tycoon games. However, the fundamental distinction is that many of these games seek to impose specific ideologies about the way systems operate. The Sims for example, can be understood as a model of capitalist ideology (Sicart, 2003). This practice in games is as old as Monopoly itself, a game designed to impart Georgist economics (Orbanes, 2006) . The history of such games is largely tied to the implementation of political ideologies or game theory.

On the other end of the spectrum are contemporary, self-identified social impact games. These games attempt to provide overt messages that are similar in character to first generation educational films. The games are often literal and their messages direct. Such games frequently ostracize their experience, leaving it at the fringes of player preferred play and interest. The games may ultimately become popular among the niche that produces and champions it. This is appropriate for developing a community around the practice, but it fails to impact those who do not know about such play or the concepts it seeks to promote.

The goal of the third generation of Critical Gameplay practice is to bridge this dichotomy in what is commonly described as procedural rhetoric (Bogost, 2010). Instead of providing overt messaging on the game's agenda, it seeks to offer fundamentally basic and inviting gameplay based on new concepts in play. The gameplay continues to embed a message through mechanic, but the mechanic is subtle. The goal is to create games that can be popular of their own right. Yet, instead of revealing themselves as social impact, players do what they naturally do – look for the fastest way to win the game. The game's message is embedded not in the explicit rules of play, but in the resulting methodological framework players derive to win.

The lesson is not in the winning or playing as instructed, but in the player's experience in discovering a better way to win.

The question the modern, digital designer must ask is how contemporary computer games utilize their larger player base to encourage players to think differently about the systems they assume on a daily basis. How can a game make people more aware of their own innate stereotypes? How can designer's help people practice becoming more open minded, or perhaps even adopt an entirely new mindset?

The Design

As a Critical Gameplay game, Black Like Me is designed around a simple premise - create games that identify the weakness in specific problem solving approaches. If games are understood as practice in problem solving, then the instruction sets and rules in games are the structure on which that practice is built. Popular games ask players to do fairly basic tasks like match similar colors, objects and patterns (e.g. match 3 games). This type of practice is not inherently philosophical. Yet, its prescription is clear. Players should seek out likeness, finding things that belong together by appearance.

Black Like Me's first layer of play works to play upon this first question. Players are asked to match one tile to another tile of the same color in a grid. As they match correctly, the game's color range is reduced until the last matches in a round are narrowly

This assumption of the match interaction, of finding similarly colored objects or discerning objects by color provides a conceptual scaffold whether intended or not. The scaffold is one which supports an oversimplified image or attribution. Like colors must be grouped. All white tiles in one section, all black tiles in another. The question to ask is what happens when that oversimplification asks players to discern the shades of grey that are inevitably true to life? Isn't the understanding of such shades one milestone in maturation as a medium as an individual? different shades of black. Where once there were many heterogeneous tiles selected out, there are now fairly homogenous tiles left. At this level, the game is practice in ambiguity and selection.

Games are also generally prescriptive in their play. Players understand a right way and a wrong way to play. In digital play, the wrong way is enforced with punishing consequence (e.g. game over, round lost, or unsupported results). Too often games are accepted as simple rule sets and players are rarely supported in critical examinations of those rule sets. Playing a shooting game as a pacifist does not disarm your opponents, it simply leaves you prey to aggressors.

Black Like Me is designed for one simple execution of critical playing. Keeping with the expectations of games that comply with Google Play and Apple App store requirements the game presents itself as a standard matching game. The match is presumably based on color, as the games instructions imply.

In reality, the game becomes impossibly difficult when players discern by color. Instead players can examine the game screen more carefully. There is a trick. The match tile may have the same color, but it also behaves differently. The last tile to appear on the screen is the tile the player wants. The difference in timing is perceptible, but in milliseconds. When the player observes this, the challenge in the game is greatly simplified. If the player stairs at the whole screen, instead of discriminating for the one single, affirming color match, the pattern becomes apparent.

This game is then about more. It is not about affirming the game mechanic - find two things alike and match them – a constant practice in classification. Instead, the game is about asking more questions of the game system. This is more than a cheat, as it is explicitly designed into the game as the true way to play. Players are rewarded not for cheating the system, but for asking a single critical question about the gameplay experience – can I play this game another way?

Conclusion

Black Like Me has proven a relative success for such alternative play. It's $.99 USD version has ranked in 9 countries on the Apple App store; Sweden, Australia, United States, Netherlands, Italy, Germany, United Kingdom, Spain and France. It has ranked in the top 100 dice or puzzle games in Sweden, Australia and the United States [5].

This distribution and sales activity is not a bragging point; it is simply a demonstration that such multilayered play has potential in the general entertainment space. The game was never billed as educational, artistic or critical. Yet, that is what it is. Players of Monopoly don't prepare themselves to engage in a Georgist rhetoric game, they engage in simple entertainment. Not every player will comprehend the message, but every player is receiving the practice in ambiguity or the revelation that the game can be beat by holistic evaluation.

In Black Like Me, the way to winning the game or getting the highest score is not through color matching, it is through ignoring color and watching for behavior. The game is designed around a revelation scenario designed to inspire thoughtful reflection in players. Revelation scenarios are meant to become pivot moments at which a player says, I remember when I thought that game was really difficult, but then I realized I was playing it the wrong way. Such practice does not support mindless adoption of rules, but instead encourages players to question the rules, not only ways in which the designer may support efficiencies (e.g. cheats).

This Critical Gameplay practice is about layering more than one set of procedural rhetoric. Players have the surface experience, which is mundane entertainment and perhaps ultimately frustrating. The second layer is one which players are rewarded for evaluating the mechanics and exploiting the weakness. Ultimately the weakness is embedded, but by so being embedded they are a designed rhetoric. Like the rhetorical structures of alliteration, simile and metaphor the player is given an opportunity to accept the experience as sounding good at the surface or querying author intention.

Black Like Me is designed to be difficult when players match tiles on color. The longer they do it, the harder it becomes. The more people learn about each other, the more they should learn that it is not the color of one's skin that is a basis for match, it is behavior. This is where the title of the game is derived. The title references the sociological experiment of a Caucasian man who colored his skin to live as an African American. Despite the praise for this kind of research, is simply pigmenting your skin a true view of life as an African American? It also references the notion of rhetorical simile, which draws parallel where parallel may not be perceived. Should you group two people who look the same, or should you ask more meaningful questions about why they belong together?

Aesthetics, whether clothes, material expression, etc are not the only means for identifying matches in grouping. Two things that seem to look alike, may not really be the same. A player's only chance is in their ability to comprehend the entire scene and find pattern. The game endeavors to drive that point home through practice without ever explicitly referencing its meaning. Not every player will comprehend the message, but every player is receiving the practice in ambiguity or the revelation that the game can be beat by holistic evaluation.

References:
[1] App Annie-App Ranking and Analytics, http://www.appannie.com/top/, last accessed September 18, 2013
[2] Bogost, I. 2010. Persuasive Games: The Expressive Power of Videogames. The MIT Press.
[3] Grace, Lindsay. "Critical games: Critical design in independent games." Proceedings of DIGRA. 2014.
[4] Grace, Lindsay. Doing Things with Games: Social Impact Through Play. CRC Press, 2019.
[5] Orbanes, P. Monopoly: The World's Most Famous Game- and how it Got that Way. Da Capo Press, 2006.
[6] Sicart, M. Family Values: Ideology, Computer Games & Sims. In 2003 DIGRA Conference, Digital Games Research Association (2003).

Section II

The Black Game Maker's Experience

Overview on Personal Narratives

Game designers, developers and others involved in making games from the African diaspora were invited to share their stories as they felt appropriate.   The following passages offer an opportunity to examine the experience of these designers without the filter of academic analysis. The following are stories and autobiographies of Black game designers and developers. The content of these have not been edited toward academic language but are instead offered in the voice of the designer.

Gordon P Bellamy

Full Professor, USC Games, CEO, Gay Gaming Professionals

With urgency I copy and pasted a reminder for others to submit their games and stories, in every Facebook group that was near the intersection of Blackness, as experienced, and gaming. Our stories must be told, and we must be accountable to tell our stories.

I made this tweet …

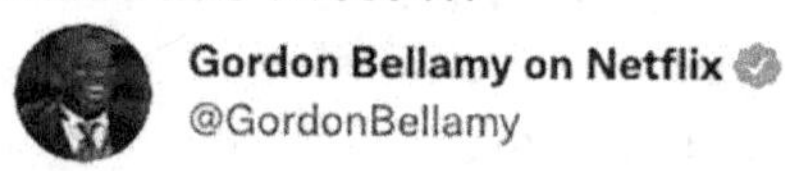

Submission Deadline Tomorrow March 15th.
@blackgamemaker1

blackgames.professorgrace.com/index.html

The Book of Black Game Makers aims to create an encyclopedic and archival record of the work of the game designs from the African diaspora. Card game or video game, commercial or academic.

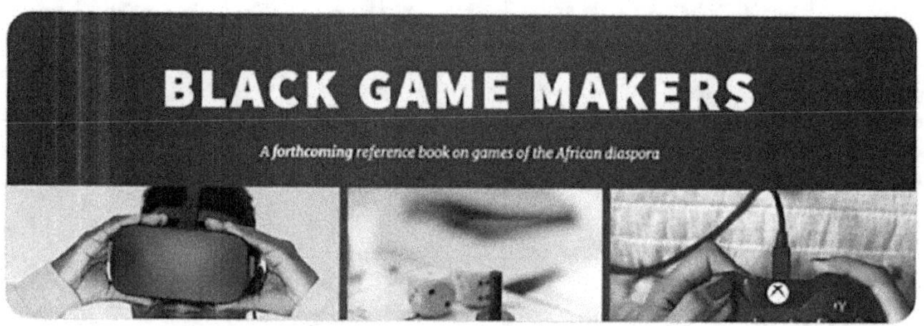

6:17 PM · Mar 13, 2021 · Twitter Web App

https://twitter.com/GordonBellamy/status/1370876749278408705 and then ran a $100 marketing campaign hoping that it might reach one more story.

And a saying that I often impart echo'd in my head. "You are too quick to give away the pizza before remembering to take a slice." I am part of the story, my Blackness is a part of our shared story in games.

My journey has taken me from Virginia to Harvard to designing Madden Football to leading both trade organizations for the entire game industry to Tencent to USC Games with many stops, joys, and pains, along the way.

I am the first ever winner of the Jerry Lawson Lifetime Achievement Award from Black in Gaming at the Game Developers Conference, I have, like the author, received the Vanguard Award from Game for Change, I was featured during Black History Month by Nickelodeon and am now preserved forever? On Netflix in the High Score Documentary and on Disney + The World According to Jeff Goldblum.

Games have always mattered to me. As a black man and a gay citizen, I was raised both explicitly and implicitly that there would be a unique set of rules that I would need to navigate in every interaction. People often speak of "the talk" the dialogue with ones parents about this topic, or "The day that you find out you are Black" , whether that be an interaction with law enforcement or some other visceral systemic bias. I'd offer that in my experience there is a continuous discourse, and that racism and other biases exist more like persistent echoes, the are an ongoing experience, whether or not, in the moment you are experiencing race, gender expression, or identity per se.

Neil Jones

Designer-developer behind Never Yield

Aerial_Knight, also known as Neil, is the designer-developer behind Never Yield. This Narrative Runner requires the player to Survive A futuristic Tokyo-style Detroit. The game focuses on it's player character, Wally, who has uncovered evidence that can change his city forever. The game combines story and runner mechanics to create a world of constant motion and persistent obstacles. Aerial_Knight reflects on his personal and professional path in game making in the following passages:

"Hi I'm Neil, I go by Aerial_Knight online and I'm the creator and developer of a game called Aerial_Knight's Never Yield". This is how I introduce myself nowadays, and it always sounds so strange to me when I say these words knowing the journey it took to get to this point, but I'm so proud to be able to say them.

Growing up I spent a lot of time outside making up random games to play with other kids who lived around me. I would play video games with my grandma from time to time, on this Sega Genesis (Weiss, 2016) that we had. We'd play Bejeweled (2001), it was her favorite game, and my favorite thing we would enjoy together. Even with that I still felt really lonely and depressed growing up. By the time I was 10 most of my family had already passed away. The older I got the more I lost, and the more I turned to video games to escape.

I wanted to create that same sense of childhood escape and joy for others. So, I decided rather young that I wanted to make games. I attended a for-profit college that offered "Game-Design" Degrees in the form of a Bachelor Of Fine Art (BFA) where I met some interesting people but I ended up teaching myself mostly. I found that I was skilled in 3D Art and environment work. I'd often be complimented on my ability to mimic art styles easily. But there was very little need for that skill set in Detroit. I spent much time searching for work in the games industry and would rarely hear back. When I did, however, it was just to thank me for my time and to let me know that they had chosen someone who was a "better fit."

Over the years of struggle and with a bit of time to reflect. The feedback I did receive when talking to recruiters and others who would review my work. The critiques were rarely about my work or my abilities, it was always more about where I lived, the lack of shipped titles, and that I may not fit the studio culture they have. This left me feeling that nothing was good enough, I needed to do better. I spent years improving and learning everything I could to only face the same result time, and time again. Over time I would meet a lot of people who had similar stories and most of them happened to look like me.

Never Yield was born out of this frustration with the games industry. I hit a point where I just didn't care anymore - I was over the whole thing. Before I would give up totally, I figured I'd take one last large swing. To prove to myself that I had always been good enough more than anything else. I decided to make a game that would truly represent me. It wouldn't matter if I was the only one who would ever play it. All that mattered was that I finished it, and it was dope. If other people enjoyed it, I would keep on this path. If not, then I would move on with my life and find another passion.

I built the prototype in my free time and would reach out to friends when I would get stuck. I had two-day jobs at the time, so I spent a lot of late nights building out the concept. I picked a runner type of game because I felt that it was a genre that hadn't really changed much over the years. That would allow me to tweak the mechanics and players would still know how it basically worked just by looking at it. The runner genre had a lot to work with, and had the added benefit of being fun to watch others play. It would give me a chance to show off my art skills and take advantage of my ability to model quickly.

After a few months, I had a level put together, a working prototype to have people play and give me some early feedback. I was surprised how much people enjoyed it, especially kids, even with the clear issues the game had. I noted the things some playtesters were having issues with in the prototype which I ended up removing or reimagining.

Overall, I was feeling really good about it. The months would focus on what made the game fun. I would remove everything that got in the way of that. While also searching for the game's sound by working with my friend Dan who had been helping with music for small projects for years. We spent almost 3 months testing out different styles of music. Eventually, landing on a mix of Jazz and Classic hip-hop type beats dawning inspiration from anime and rap. This turned out to be a very good choice in the long run. It gave the game a heartbeat that you could feel while playing it.

Through the process of creating Aerial_Knight's Never Yield, I did mostly everything from the art, design, marketing, to cutting the trailers. Because if people didn't like a certain aspect of what I was making then it would be 100% on me and the choices I made, no one else's. I put my name in the title of the game as a constant reminder of this ideal.

2 years after the original prototype the game is set to release on the PS4/PS5, Xbox x|s, Nintendo Switch, Steam, & Epic Games Store. The biggest takeaway from the whole process is something my high school gym coach used to always say every class, "things don't change they remain the same unless you change it." I don't know why I remembered it so many years later but I thought about it often during the development of the game.

References:
98

- Bejeweled. PopCap Games, 2001
- Weiss, Brett. Classic Home Video Games, 1989-1990: A Complete Guide to Sega Genesis, Neo Geo and TurboGrafx-16 Games. McFarland, 2016.

They were wrong about me they can be wrong about you

Jonathan Herman Jennings

I didn't know what programming actually was when I enrolled in my game development program. I couldn't tell you what a variable was, or a function, I vaguely understood games involved some kind of assembly language, some complicated pattern of 0's and 1's. Still, I knew that IF programming and code would somehow help me to be able to make a game then it was worth trying to learn.

This is after years of being told my math skills were too weak and I'd have to do much better if I was ever going to program games for a living. Boy, those teachers were right, and that curriculum was way above my head. The most important professor of my academic career, Professor Randall Maynes, stated to all of his students if we needed extra time to study after class he'd stay until 5 and class typically ended around 3. I stayed after class a lot and still managed to be a pretty middle of the road student I just had a hard time grasping abstract concepts and my brain literally would hurt at the end of class some days as I tried to struggle with algorithms, discrete mathematics, physics calculations, and bubble sorts. Then one day my brain broke.

Somehow all the programming gibberish started to come together, I was never the strongest student technically. I was not the model student who could whip up a lightning-quick sorting algorithm and you'd never want me to program your AI at that young age but what I did have was a vision for games. To me making a game was like cooking the game concept and code itself being the core of the dish and a generous seasoning of audio, art, pretty UI, and great storytelling helping to pull all the flavors together and make something you can enjoy until you've devoured every bite. Most colleges don't test for game design vision though and they especially do it in a programming curriculum so I continued to be a B-student who grappled with code to try to learn how to make those visions come true.

The only people that cared less for my game design vision paired with very rudimentary junior programmer skills less than my college were the studios and odd jobs I applied to. The game industry today is made up of roughly 2% black people so you can imagine nearly 10 years ago how shocked the mostly white faces I interviewed with must have been to see a young black man applying for their junior game programmer position. I recall showing up at a studio and the secretary asking me if I was there to drop off a package when I was there for the junior game programmer interview. I recall the oddly tense and awkward questioning I'd get when a programming interviewer wanted to know how my black mind learned how to write code … obviously I was out of my depth. I recall when I was looking for a temporary job in my junior year of college and how the interviewer went from supportive and caring to spiteful and negative about my idiotic pursuit for a games career after I laid out the challenges that laid on the road ahead of me " You have just told me that it is a highly competitive industry where people like you don't make it, we'll be here when it doesn't work out". Lots of rejections and I was never sure if it was because I'm black, a bad programmer, or both ?!

Then one day someone decided to roll the dice on me they needed someone to help with the project and I was only too hungry to offer my assistance. Even that first team though I recall them comparing in hushed tones me a college-educated black man with a degree in Game programming to a coworker who dropped out of college and had been interning for months " Whose the better programmer you think?". It was a brief debate that ended in a stalemate.

I've been in the industry for 9 years now I have been a guest speaker at multiple colleges, been a speaker at conferences, have worked on dozens of published titles, my work has seen millions of downloads and even some of the games I have worked on have been rated pretty well (plenty of credit extended to the awesome teams I've been on). I have just wrapped up a solo project I developed for a VR game incubator called Oculus Launchpad in which I competed against 100 talented creators selected from around the globe for the chance to be awarded a grant to complete my game vision and lead a project.

My point in sharing all of this is that on my road I have been told constantly that the Games Industry is not for a person like me. This dark skin causes them to underestimate my brain and as my momma taught me we have to work twice as hard to be considered just as good and that mentality has allowed me chances even some of my white colleague's envy. I had an ex-coworker flippantly call me an "F-ing Diversity Hire" undermining all the hard hours of study and work that got me to my current position in life. What I have found is that people love to tell you why you can't be successful especially when you're black. My response to that is simple though if they were wrong about me then they can be wrong about you. I hope that every strong black soul who won't let their dreams die and has read this gets to relish the sweet echoes of " you'll never make it" that never came true. The number of people who tell me they knew I'd make it but scoffed when I mentioned my ambitions. If they were wrong about me then they can be wrong about you.

Boris Willis

Faculty, George Mason University

If I had my way, I would have started in the band in 6th grade as a drummer instead of a trumpet player, but my mom would not be convinced. Drumming dreams dashed, I pressured my parents into buying me a computer and although I wanted a Commodore 64, we settled on an Atari 400 because of its price. It was not a good compromise, but I was able to get some understanding of programming by making my name to move across the screen on the diagonal. Also, the vastly improved graphics on the Atari 400 compared to the Atari 2600 excited me about the possibilities of computers for the future. I remember my mom and sister taking classes in Fortran, but I never got to take any programming lessons. I instead devoted myself to dance. It was the first time I worked hard to achieve something. I had to make my body flexible, strong and articulate which was a challenge I enjoyed. I went to college for dance and never saw a computer on campus at the North Carolina School of the Arts as it was called then. However, I was drawn to the technology of sound, Ken Nordine and his Word Jazz, Charles Amirkhanian and his sound poetry, John Cage, and his use of chance and the world of musique concrète. I made audio recordings on a regular basis, spliced tape from my cassettes to make new music and embodied the singing style of Bobby McFerrin as I was no good at beat boxing.

In college I loved dance improvisation class the most. The ability to just move and allow the intelligence of my body to overtake the careful considerations of my brain was thrilling. I was always a bit of a physical daredevil. You might have seen me rolling off of my roof, making ramps to jump over things with my bike or walking on barrels as fast as I could. While I did nothing specifically involving technology in school, I was fascinated by surrealism in art especially the work of Salvador Dali. Hearing Ken Nordine's soundscapes seemed like the audio version of Dali's work. When I looked at a

Dali painting, I always saw something new, and I could listen to Word Jazz I heard something different every time. My senior piece was called the Sound Museum and it was based on a Word Jazz segment from Ken Nordine, and it used recordings by Nordine and Bobby McFerrin as well as Annea Lockwood's sound piece, Tiger Balm. Ultimately, it was not the success that I had hoped for, but it laid to foundation for me to create surrealist performances, and eventually the surreal elements of game worlds.

After college, I met John Simmons while teaching dance at George Mason University. Simmons had created a way to create and send animations via a Netscape web browser with the 3D VRML application Cosmo Player. Instead of just chatting with text, Simmons imagined that you could trade movement phrases in what he called "humanizing the web." To do this, he wanted to use Labanotation, a notation system invented by Rudolf Von Laban which is used in dance to describe and record movement and spacial pathways using symbols. Simmons called his program Animated Dance Event Language or ADEL. I worked with him on building and defining the flexible limits of a 3d model who we named Aadelle and set up some constraints on her movement based on what my body could do. The animations could move to and from different positions by creating poses on a timeline or inputting numbers that would determine the rotation of her joints. We created a dance called *Sirob and Aadelle-Boolean Netscape Remix in Denied Space*. In this performance work, Simmons animated a 3D model in real-time showing how removing the limitations of gravity created weightless movement possibilities and I performed in contrast to show how gravity created impactful movement possibilities. Working with Simmons kick started my interest in moving in 3D space. In the dance community, there was lots of buzz about chorographer Merce Cunningham's use of Life Forms, which was later called Dance Forms for his choreography. I had the opportunity to test out the software, but I remember it being difficult to use and I was curious about animating with motion capture.

The ability to put my choreography into a computer with motion capture and create an application around it was inspiring. When I applied to graduate schools, they had to be actively using motion capture. For my final graduate project, I created what I called a live video game. It combined a game show, dance, theater, used video and the music was composed and played in real-time by my friend David Morneau on a Nintendo Gameboy. I produced, performed, and choreographed the story of an evil artistic director who was turning his dancers into *choreobots*. The choreobots were digital animated versions of the dancers that were connected to and powered by their human selves. The director could work them as long and as hard as he wanted. It was the job of the audience to play different games that would free the dancers and get them to the theater so they could perform as their fully human selves. When the dancers arrived at the theater, they were whisked away to a website where their adventures and the games continued. The idea was to keep the audience involved in the performance and continue to develop the work with a built-in audience for future shows.

I recently began posting some of the game related parts of my performance work on itch.io. I enjoy the ability to create and play in game worlds and on stage and bring dance and games together as often as I can. Currently, I have three works posted, The Owl, The Fish, The Maiden and He, an interactive poem that challenges the player to figure out the correct order of the words while occasionally getting interrupted by another story of a police officer killing an unarmed Black person. Natasha: A Game of Dance, is a dance adventure game made with DC based dance group Company E and Dots, a lighting and spacing visualization for a dance I created on dancers at Keene College in New Hampshire in January 2020 but never got to perform because of the Covid-19 pandemic.

I continue to perform and create performance-based work mainly in Unreal Engine and as the technology evolves, I will be there tinkering with the possibilities and dancing in the surreal world of games.

■**Black Game Studies**

On creating Home R Where The Heart Is

Blake Andrews

For the Global Game Jam in 2019, the theme was what home means to you. I saw a lot more serious/narrative games that year. It felt like a bad idea because people will probably ""not go all the way"" in terms of a dark or serious narrative, or go part of the way just to be evocative
or to be real twee or whatever. Though, some of the games that I had liked this year were the more heart warming ones.

At home, when my family celebrates Christmas, we put a black Santa on top of the tree. I found out recently that my grandma painted him black so he would look like my grandpa.

The sprites in the game are the Konami Simpsons arcade beat em up. The characters are altered from having yellow skin to brown to look of African decent. This is in reference to the history of black Bart bootleg memorabilia popular in the 90's which I find to be a parallel with my black Santa.

In many of these bootleg shirts there will be multiple black Barts all crowding around. Sometimes these feature stereotypes of black culture like Bart hitting on a woman with a big butt. One of my favorites was my former roommate's boyfriend's shirt that she would wear. It had multiples of different looking Barts on a roller coaster which said "Bébé's Kids". Bébé's Kids is a 90's animated comedy about a black family that doesn't look anything similar to the Simpsons. I am interested in the uncanny quality of the pop culture mashups represented in this shirt.

In the Konami Simpsons arcade beat em up, when the Simpsons touch each other, sometimes they do team attacks. The majority of team attacks have been left unedited outside of changing the color of their skin. In place of Homer and Bart's team attack, I added an animation of Homer strangling Bart. While looking through the sprites ripped from

The Spriters Resource I was surprised that this classic motif from the Simpsons cartoon, of Homer strangling Bart, was not in the arcade game at all. I included it not only as an homage to the cartoon, but as a personal response to the Global Game Jam's thematic suggestion.

The sounds are primarily from click team fusion's free sound library with the exception of a vocal recording of "fuck off mom".

The interaction is simple, mash space or touch the screen in order to make the home disappear and reappear. Each time it reappears a group of black Simpsons, furniture, and other environmental elements. fall into the home. When it disappears, the Simpsons and other objects fall. If the player rapidly switches the house off and on the game becomes a cacophony of animation and sound effects. If you do not do anything for a while you can see birds fly around the screen chirping and can look at procedurally placed cloud homes.

On Making the Run Around:

iThrive Games Seed Institute

The Run Around is a game designed by youth who have lived experience in the justice system or Department of Youth Services (or both). It is designed to (1) highlight inequities of those systems in supporting the mental health and thriving of youth of color, and (2) dismantle unjust systems. The Run Around represents some of the thoughts, feelings, and choices the youth designers had while incarcerated or on probation or parole—frustration, boredom, lack of purpose, and absence of agency. The game is a tool to raise awareness of these experiences and initiate conversations about systems change for social justice.

The audience for The Run Around is adult stakeholders who play a role in the cradle-to-prison pipeline, including educators, law enforcement, social workers, and other community members, as well as other youth (14 and older) who may be caught in, on the verge of entering, or who bear witness to the cradle-to-prison pipeline. The designers created The Run Around to educate, transform, and challenge perceptions and attitudes about youth who are or have been involved in the justice system. The game includes real stories and experiences of youth who are victims of the cradle-to-prison pipeline, as well as statistics reflecting the racial inequities within the juvenile justice and foster care systems. Specifically, The Run Around was designed to:

- increase empathy for youth who are in the cradle-to-prison pipeline;
- increase awareness of and knowledge about the inequities and lack of support for youth who are in the cradle-to-prison pipeline; and
- increase motivation and commitments to break the systems that propel the cycle of - incarceration and institutionalization amongst youth of color.

The designers of The Run Around started their design process identifying the emotions they wanted players to feel while playing, specifically boredom, frustration, and anger—the emotions they themselves felt while in prison and while trying to understand the rules of parole. The design of the CHOICE card deck is such that it takes many rounds before players are able to move from Maximum Security to Minimum Security to Parole (only specific CHOICE cards enable a player to reduce their security level and be released, and there are just a few of those cards in the deck). While Home seems to be so close upon being released from Prison, in fact, players need to do a full lap around the board to get Home. What's more, they can only get Home if they draw the exact number from the CHOICE deck needed to enter. If they don't get the exact number, they need to remain on parole and do another lap around the board. The board is full of TRAP spaces impacting the likelihood that they will get Home. When players land on a TRAP space, they must draw a TRAP card, which will either make them lose a turn, go back 3 spaces, or go back to Prison. These design elements represent the designers' experience, that being released from prison doesn't make you free or safe; many, many obstacles remain in your pathway.

The board also includes recent statistics showing that in the United States, people of color are the most subjected to the cradle-to-prison pipeline. And, getting caught up in the pipeline starts early. For example, players learn from the board that children of color in preschools are significantly more likely to get suspended than their white peers. The designers created the character game pieces to look like themselves and people they know, and they wrote bios for each character based on their own lived experiences or those of people they know or knew.

To encourage players to reflect on these different elements of the game, the CHOICE card deck includes DISCUSS cards, which pose questions written by the designers to prompt players to notice and talk about the game and the designers' intentions. All of these elements come together to connect players to the lives of the designers and become aware of the injustices of the justice system, and the lack of support and compassion within the system to care for the youth who are at its mercy.

The win state of The Run Around is nearly impossible to attain, just like winning within the system that underlies the cradle-to-system is impossible to attain. Neither is designed for the "players" within it to win. We suggest players play for 30-60 minutes with discussion occurring during gameplay as prompted by the game mechanics

Patricia Bobo

SVP of Operations, Black Card Revoked

Latesha Williams and Jay Bobo first met when their careers brought them to Lebron James' marketing agency. They were fascinated by follower engagement on social media and saw the power and potential of Black Twitter. They exchanged hilarious Black Twitter moments and asked - "Is there a game fueled by Twitter content?" It didn't exist - yet.

The two fused their love of hip-hop and Black culture with Jay's technical skills and Latesha's marketing skills, added the operations skills of third co-founder Patricia Bobo, and in 2015, Black Card Revoked was born.

Lamont A. Harrell, II

CEO & Founder, Black Game Maker's Association

In 2017 the Black Game Makers Association founded as a way to provide resources to Black Game Designers. This commitment came from a desire to address disparities in the gaming market. In a multi-billion dollar industry in the US only two percent of those employed in the video game industry are black designers and there is even less representation when it comes to analog games in big box stores and in national gaming conventions.

BGMA advocates for Black game makers in the traditional industry, provides educational opportunities, as well as curate a space for consumers to find their work through our website www.Buyblack.games. Pulling together a strong group of Black game designers has been our way of helping to build black wealth and addressing economic disparities in this country. We look forward to helping to grow the gaming space in a way that welcomes everyone. Change The Game, Lamont A. Harrell, II

Section III

Index of Black Games

Alphabetical Games list by Title:

- Aerial_Knight's Never Yield | Neil Jones (Aerial_Knight)
- An Innovative Matrix Game to Improve Cognitive Skills, Abstract Reasoning, Problem Solving and Computational Practices | G.I.A. Mobile, Inc.
- Artifacts II | Phazero
- BCFX, The Black College Football Xperience | Nerjyzed Entertainment
- Black Card Revoked | CFAP Holdings LLC
- Black Like Me | Mindtoggle
- Black Movie Guess Quiz | Lamar Harris
- Blerd Domination | Blerd Domination
- Bushido | On the table
- Cangaço | Casa do Goblin and Bureau de Juegos
- Earth Cipher | MediaBreeze Multimedia
- Election Day | The Game, Clay Street Marketing, LLC.
- FiQuestions|Financial IQ, LLC
- Galactic Bar Fight | Weird Kid Studios
- Healer|Critical Gameplay
- Home R Where The Heart Is|everythingstaken
- HTOWN FIGHT MINNIES |Urban Tek CGI
- Inequality-opoly: The Board Game of Structural Racism and Sexism in America|Perry Clemons
- Karaoke Kards |Katrina Mickle
- La Muerte|Casa do Goblin e Sherlock SA
- Objectif|A.M. Darke, Cargo Collective
- Operator|University of Southern California
- Pull Your Card Music Trivia: Hip Hop Edition|Pull Your Card
- Rap Godz|Board Game Brothas
- Rite in Rolls|illest Preacha & Rmablin Intelluct
- Run Die Run Again|RetroNinja Inc.

- SPILL IT Card Game|SPILL IT Card Game
- Street Team: Reign of the Iron Dragon|Street Team Studios
- Super High Dunk|Eyedrinox Games
- Super Stick Skirmish of Superb Scrappers|Mecha Destroyer JD
- Systemic Lives|Digital Daydream
- The 1998 Deck|Ordinary Genius Llc.
- The Ice Cold RPG|Roaring Lions Productions
- The Run Around|iThrive Games' SEED Institute
- The Ultimate Clap Back|Mot & Dot LLC
- Trading Races|Kenyatta Forbes
- University of Dope™|Vance Hall LLC
- UnStuck|Indefinite Village
- When I Get Free (WIGF)|The Books Of Egu

Aerial_Knight's Never Yield

Released: 2021
Windows PC, XBOX, Nintendo Wii

By: Neil Jones (solo project)
Detroit, Michigan

STORY
Take the role of Wally. A mysterious character that has recovered what was taken from him. Hopefully, you're fast enough to outrun your enemies. Expose the truth and try to uncover the mystery of what happened to them.

GAMEPLAY
Aerial_Knight's Never Yield is a 3D side-scroller that plays much like a classic endless runner. The game has an interesting story that keeps players always in motion. Run, Jump, Slide or "Dash" for acrobatic variants leading to dope combinations and avoid the challenges that await. Aerial_Knight's Never Yield is being built for players who love to speedrun games while being an experience that casual players will enjoy as well.

SOUNDTRACK
This Soundtrack for Aerial_Knight's Never Yield was done by "Danime-Sama" a Detroit artist with vocals from artists all over the world.

Press:
Twinfinite.net:
https://twinfinite.net/2020/06/aerial-knights-never-yield/

IndieBloom:
http://indiebloom.co.uk/2020/09/27/run-around-a-futuristic-tokyo-style-detroit-with-aerial_knights-never-yield-next-gen-video-game/

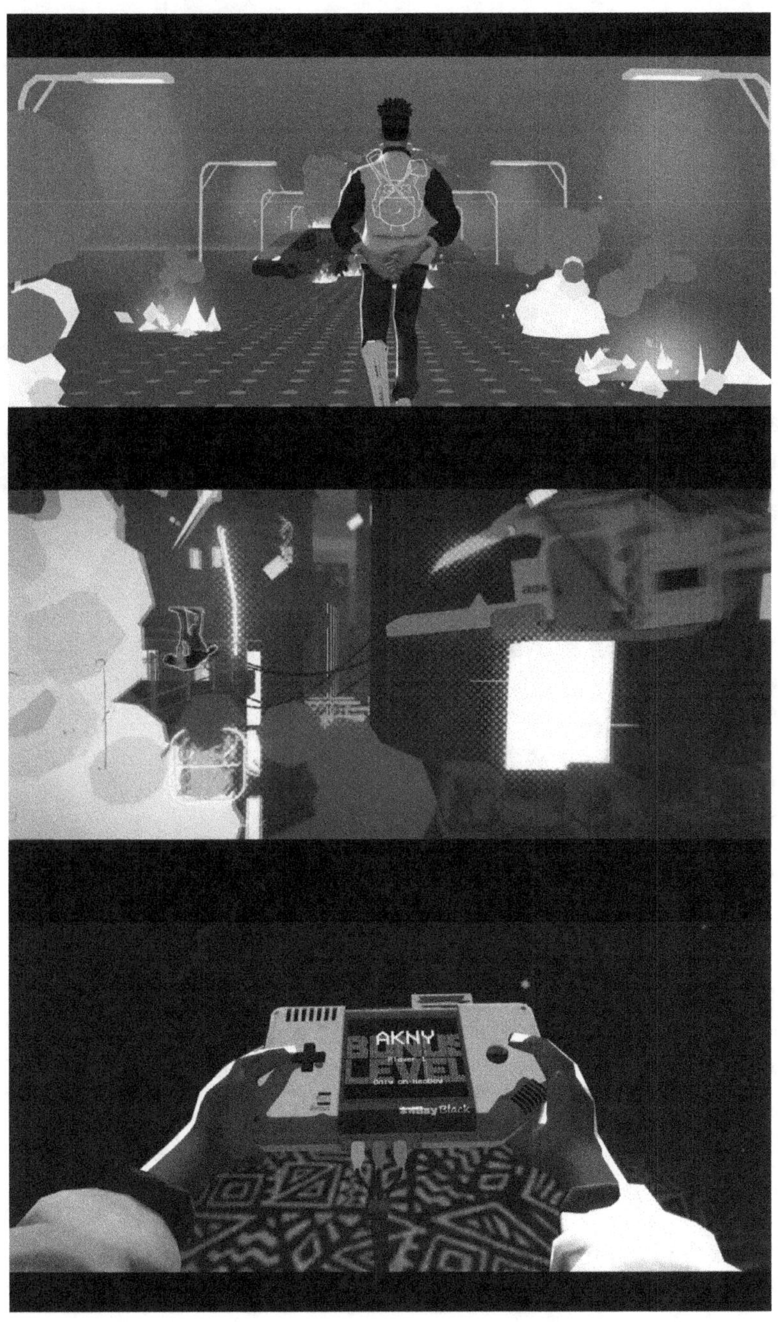
AKNY
BONUS
LEVEL
only on Radboy
GameBoy Black

Conquest IQ

Released: 2015
Digital Game: Mobile: Android, Virtual Reality
http://conquestiq.com/

By: G.I.A. Mobile, Inc.
Harlem, New York

CONQUEST IQ ® is a dual-player mobile game on a 9 x 8 matrix with new strategic moves. Each player has an Emperor, Empress, Palace Guards, Catapults, Bowmen and Foot Soldiers. It has designated areas for a River, Battlefield and Palaces. The objective is to capture the opponent's Emperor through strategic positioning. The gameplay is to entice novice and skilled matrix board players.

In terms of originality, the game maximizes the concept appeal with:
- Illustration & Animation,
- Interactive Dual-Player Platform
- Intelligible User Interface (UI) & User Experience (UX)
- Achievement & Leaderboard
- Strong Play Patterns
- Live Challenges
- Overall Design.

Awards:

2020 Games for Change Alcove Challenge Honorable Mention:
    https://youtu.be/RMy6kOrQClM

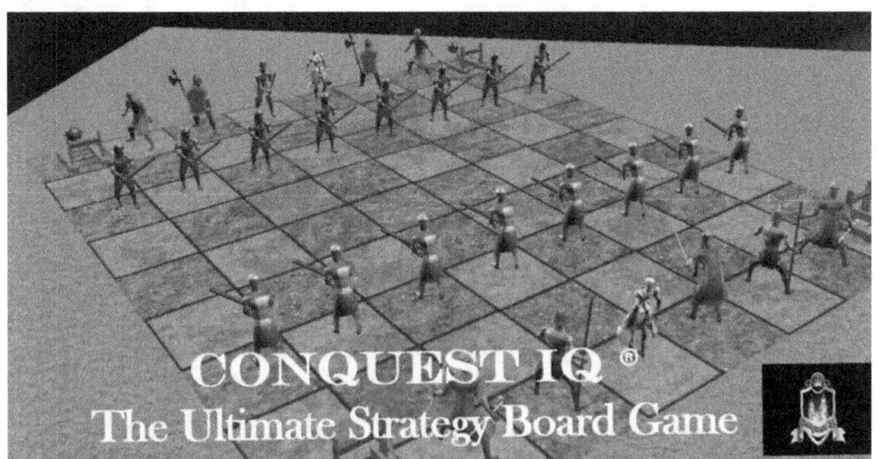
CONQUEST IQ ®
The Ultimate Strategy Board Game

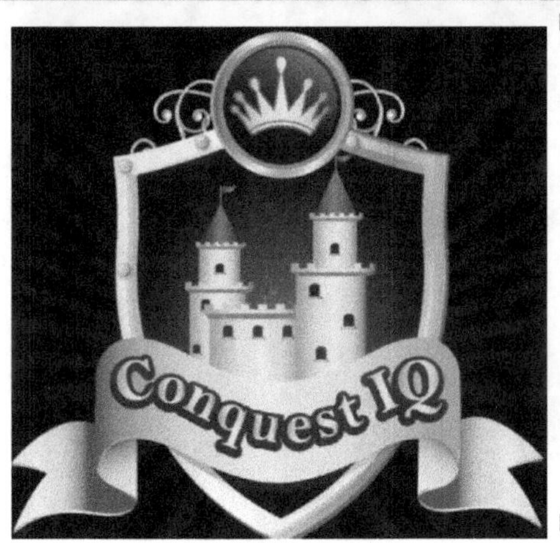
Conquest IQ

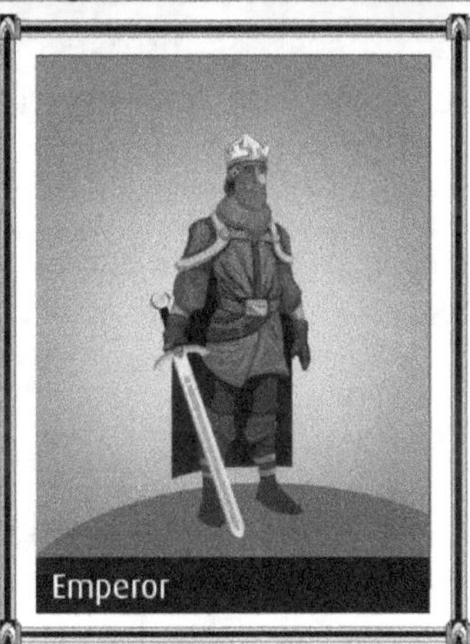
Emperor

Artifacts II

2018
Digital Game: Virtual, Augmented or Mixed Reality
http://www.christinazero.com/artifacts-ii.html

By: Phazero, Christina "Phazero" Curlee
Los Angeles, CA

Artifacts II is a single player, narrative-traversal game set in a surreal environment representing memory spaces in the character's mind.

The game is about the entanglement of trauma in the mind and body, and a process of introspection and self-evaluation occurring with someone that realizes that they are hurting and that they have hurt others due to their own pain.

Artifacts II uses elements of exploration (or walking sims), RPG, and Survival MDA to reveal the fragments of a character's broken past.

Notable Exhibitions and Presentations:
IndieCade 2018:
https://www.indiecade.com/2018-games/artifacts-ii-jacaranda/

Eyeo Festival 2019:
http://eyeofestival.com/2019/speaker/christina-phazero-curlee/

Gray Area Festival 2021:
https://grayareafestival.io/bio/phazero/

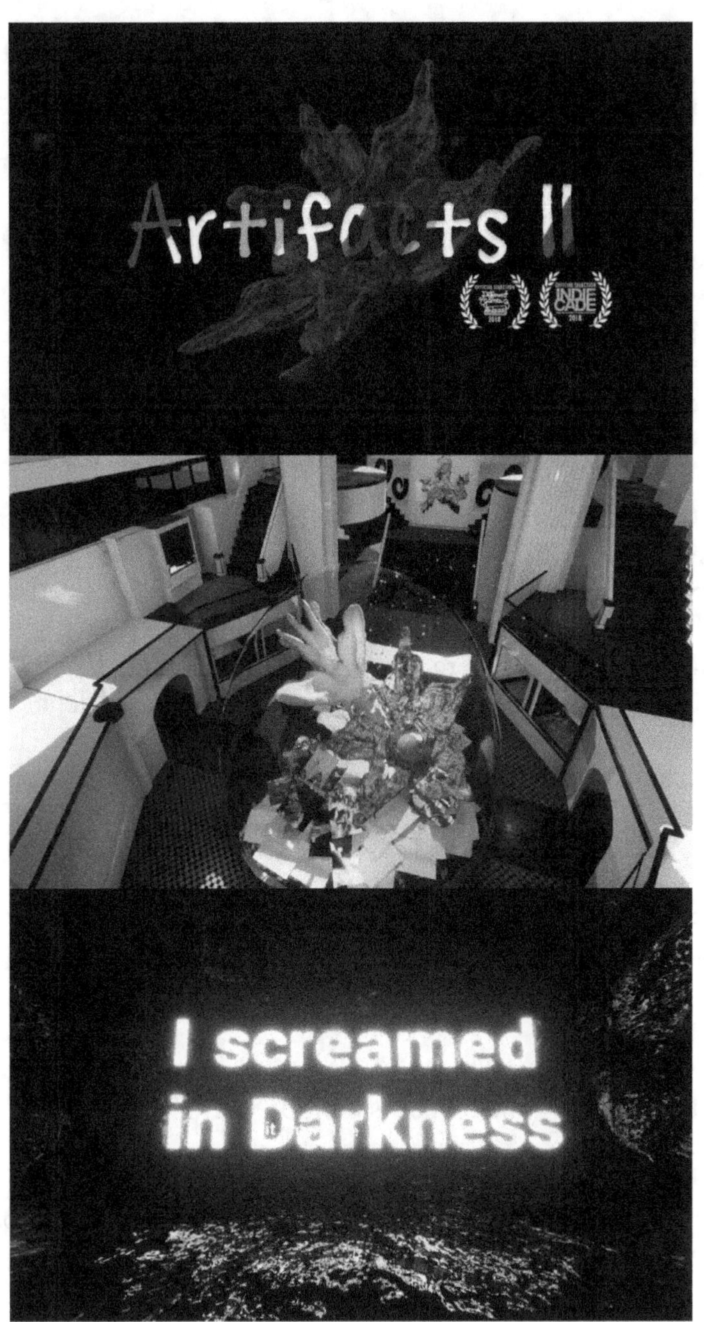
Artifacts II
I screamed
in Darkness

BCFX, The Black College Football Xperience

Released: 2007
Digital Game: Xbox 360 Console

By: Nerjyzed Entertainment
Creative Design Director: Jacqueline Beauchamp
Baton Rouge, Louisiana

Black College Football Experience (BCFx) is a sports video game centered on the culture of black college football.

Black College Football Experience (BCFx) is a sports video game centered on the culture of black college football. BCFx was created by Nerjyzed Entertainment, Inc., of Baton Rouge, LA.[2] It features Historically Black Colleges & University (HBCU) football teams from three HBCU conferences including the SWAC, SIAC, and several schools within the MEAC as well as independent HBCUs. The game features nearly 40 teams, bands, interactive halftime shows, stadiums, play-by-play commentary, and ten Classic games such as the Turkey Day Classic, Bayou Classic, Florida Classic, Atlanta Football Classic and the Southern Heritage Classic. BCFx was released on Windows-based PC systems in November 2007. An Xbox 360 version titled "The Doug Williams Edition" was released September 29.

Notable:
First game published on the XBox 360 by an African American Owned Company. The owner is an HBCU grad.

Press:
https://www.ign.com/articles/2009/10/19/black-college-football-the-experience-the-doug-williams-edition-review

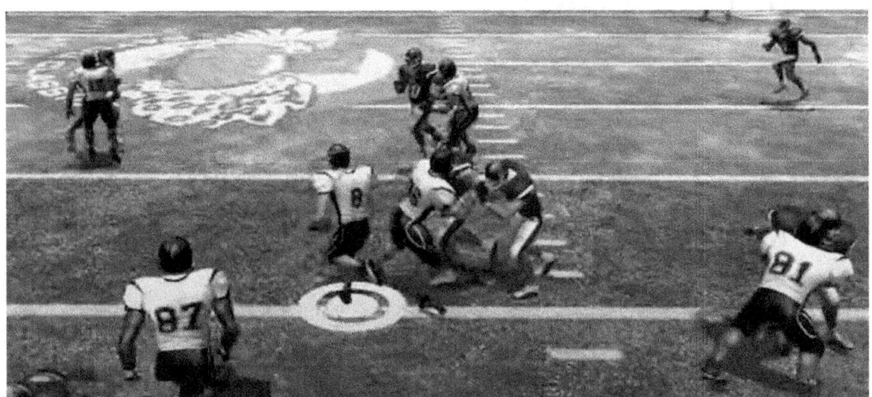

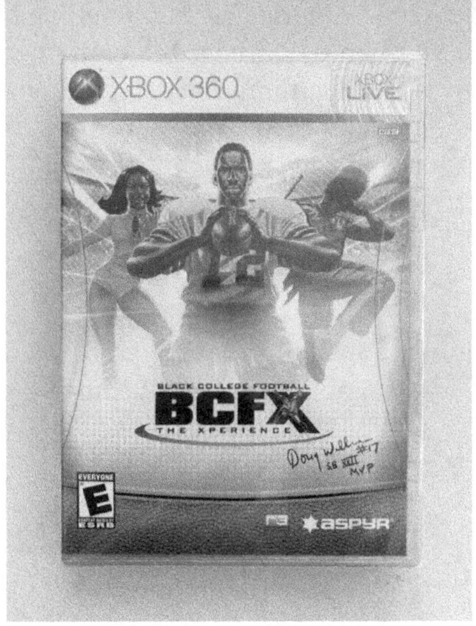

Black Card Revoked

Released: 2015
Analog game: card game

By: CFAP Holdings LLC
Columbus, Ohio

A humorous exploration, Black Card Revoked connects the masses to American black pop culture with love, peace and soul.

From the game maker:
Black Card Revoked is America's #1 best-selling black culture trivia game series sold nationwide. It is a celebration of Black American traditions, history and culture. The suite of games includes its popular expansion packs "Saved & Sanctified," "Black History," "Old School," "Jollof & Fufu" and others.

Notable Press:

LA Times:
https://www.latimes.com/california/story/2020-03-06/journee-to-inclusion-for-whittier-colleges-black-student-populace-begins-with-one-student

BizJournals:
https://www.bizjournals.com/columbus/news/2020/12/03/columbus-card-game-company-diversity.html

Oprah.com
https://www.oprah.com/gift/oprahs-favorite-things-2020-black-card-revoked?editors_pick_id=78562

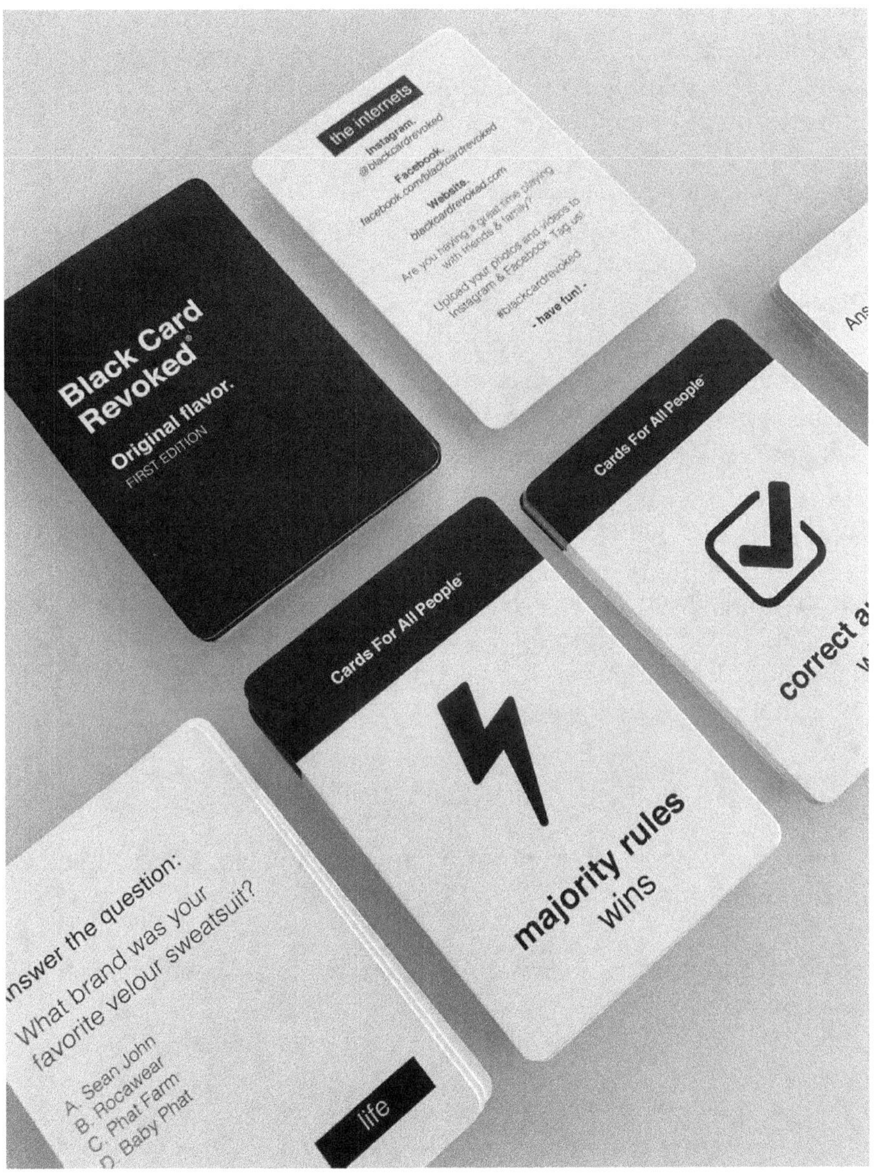
the internets
Instagram.
@blackcardrevoked
Facebook.
facebook.com/blackcardrevoked
Website.
blackcardrevoked.com
Are you having a great time playing with friends & family?
Upload your photos and videos to Instagram & Facebook. Tag us!
#blackcardrevoked
- have fun! -

Black Card Revoked
Original flavor.
FIRST EDITION

Cards For All People

Cards For All People

Cards For All People

correct a

majority rules
wins

Answer the question:
What brand was your favorite velour sweatsuit?
A. Sean John
B. Rocawear
C. Phat Farm
D. Baby Phat

life

Ans

Black Like Me

Released: 2013
Digital Game: Apple iOS, Android and HTML 5
https://criticalgameplay.com/games/BlackLikeMe/

By: Mindtoggle (Lindsay Grace)
Washington, DC

Players are asked to match one tile to another tile of the same color in a grid. As they match correctly, the game's color range is reduced until the last matches in a round are narrowly different shades of black. Where once there were many heterogeneous tiles selected out, there are now fairly homogenous tiles left.

In reality, the game becomes impossibly difficult when players discern by color. Instead players can examine the game screen more carefully. There is a trick. The match tile may have the same color, but it also behaves differently. If the player stairs at the whole screen, instead of discriminating for the one single, affirming color match, the pattern becomes apparent.

Notable:

Top 10 daily ranks on Apple App store for Puzzle and Dice games in 2 countries

Top 100 daily ranks on Apple App store for Puzzle and Dice games in 4 countries

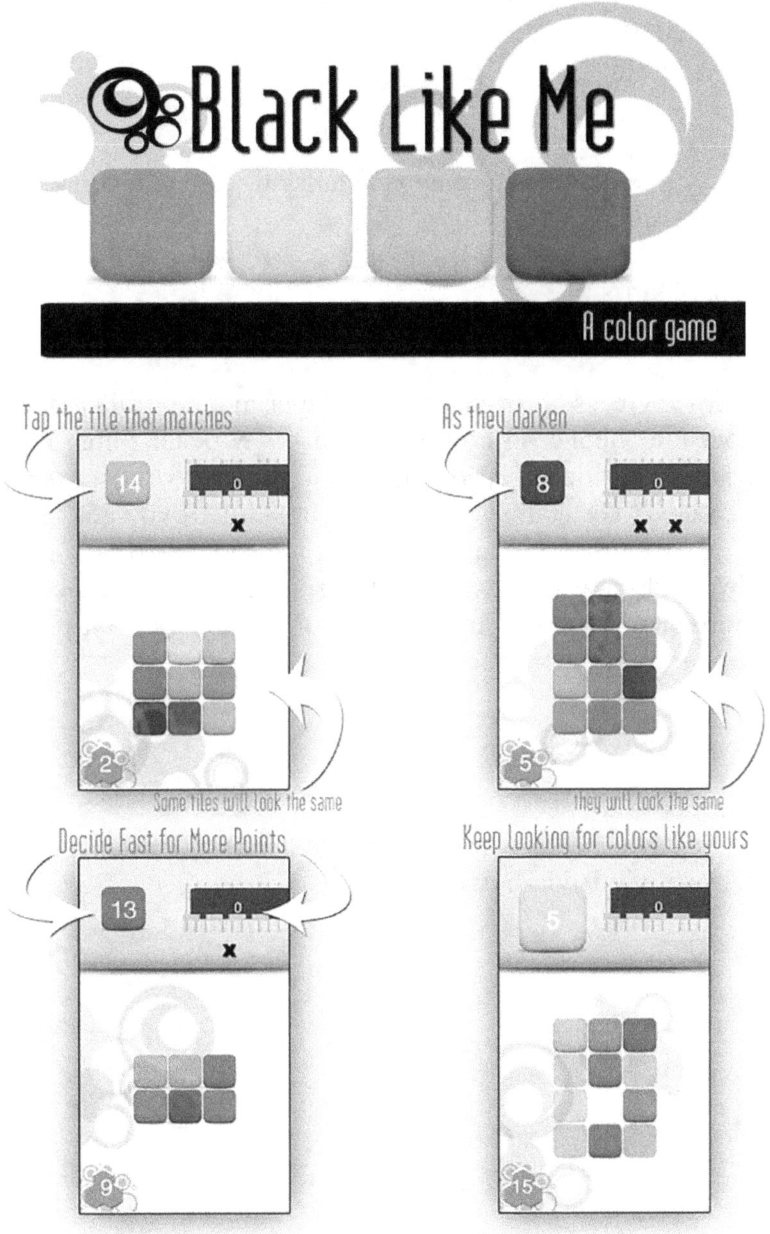

Tap the tile that matches

Some tiles will look the same

As they darken

they will look the same

Decide Fast for More Points

Keep looking for colors like yours

Black Movie Guess Quiz
Released: 2019
Mobile: Android

URL:
https://play.google.com/store/apps/details?id=com.cincyquiz.black
movieguessquiz

By: Lamar Harris
Cincinnati, Ohio

Black Movie Guess Quiz, is a single-player mobile trivia game that tests your knowledge on how well you know black films. Players can guess the movie based on an artistic drawing of a scene. The game features over 100 levels to test your skills. If you get stuck on a level, you can use your coins to access hints to help or ask a friend for help by sharing on Facebook Messenger. You earn a coin for every correct answer. If you run out of coins, there are multiple ways for you to earn additional coins

Notable Press:

BlackNews.com:
https://www.blacknews.com/news/lamar-harris-mobile-gaming-app-black-movie-trivia-nostalgia/

■Black Game Studies

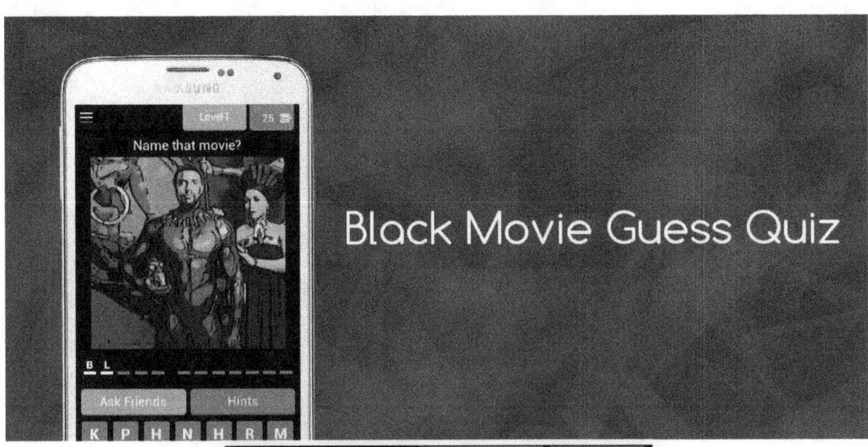

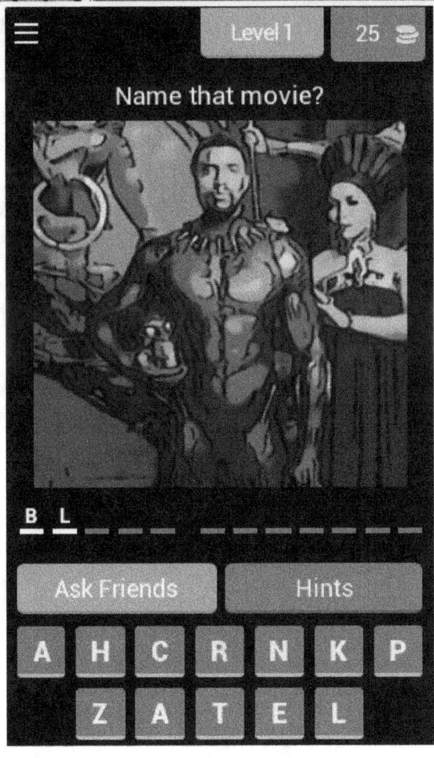

Blerd Domination

Released: 2020
Board, Card or other analog game,
Mac OS, Android, iOS, Windows XP, VISTA, or 7, Windows 8
www.blerddomination.com

By: Blerd Domination
Maryland

A fun trivia game celebrating Blerd culture, whether you're into fandoms, sports, music, pop culture, history, or politics, there's something for you. Can also be used as a learning tool in-lieu of flashcards for learning, homeschool, and supplementing school curriculums.

Blerd Domination Trivia Card Game Contents:

> Card dimensions: 87 X 56mm 198 Total Cards 1 instruction card 24 Answer Cards 154 Trivia Questions + "Hard Mode" "Let's Fight" (Debate) Cards

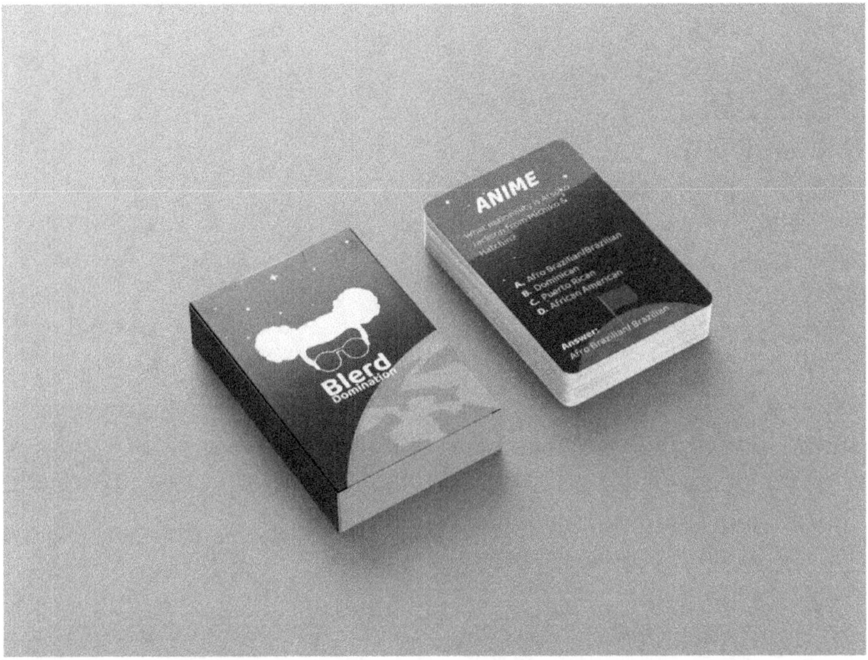

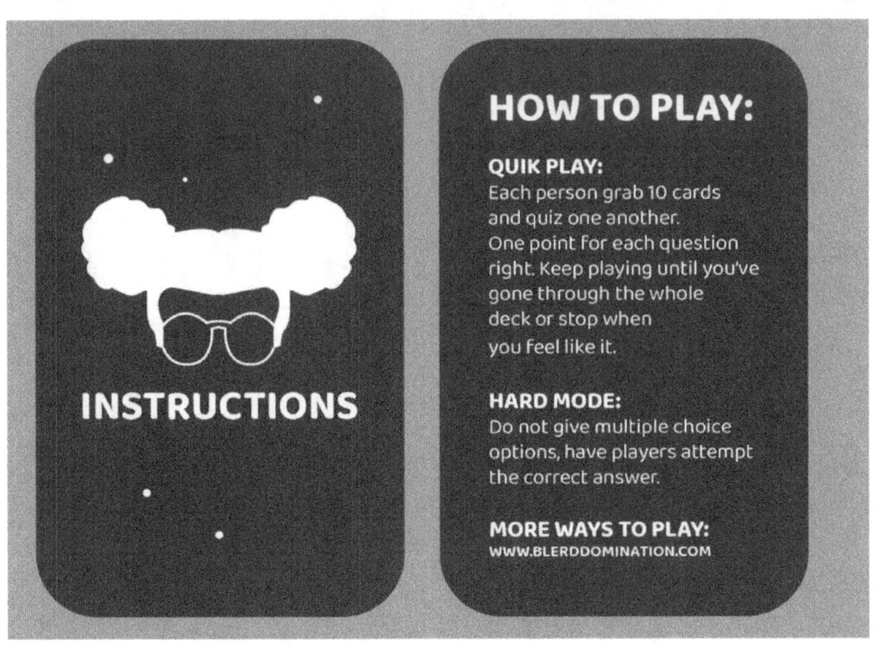

ANIME

A. Afro Brazilian/Brazilian
B. Dominican
C. Puerto Rican
D. African American

Answer:
Afro Brazilian/ Brazilian

Blerd
Domination

INSTRUCTIONS

HOW TO PLAY:

QUIK PLAY:
Each person grab 10 cards
and quiz one another.
One point for each question
right. Keep playing until you've
gone through the whole
deck or stop when
you feel like it.

HARD MODE:
Do not give multiple choice
options, have players attempt
the correct answer.

MORE WAYS TO PLAY:
WWW.BLERDDOMINATION.COM

Bushido

Released: 2019
Board, Card or other analog game
www.ludopedia.com.br/jogo/bushido

By: On the Table
Mesquita/RJ, Brazil

Samurai were the most prominent individuals in Japanese society during Feudal Japan. Proud and respected, their lives were a journey of devotion to the arts of war and dueling, with the warrior's path, Bushido, as their code of conduct. In Bushido, go back in time during the era of shoguns and daimios and assume the role of a samurai warrior who will fight to defend the honor of his clan through the sword, in a game of deduction, tactics and concentration, where a wrong move can cost life.

Combine your cards and confuse your opponent so that he is not able to predict your next move, either in attack or defense. Your reputation and your honor as a samurai warrior are in your hands!

Press:
https://turnoextrabg.com.br/2020/05/13/top-d6-jogos-acessiveis-para-2-jogadores/"

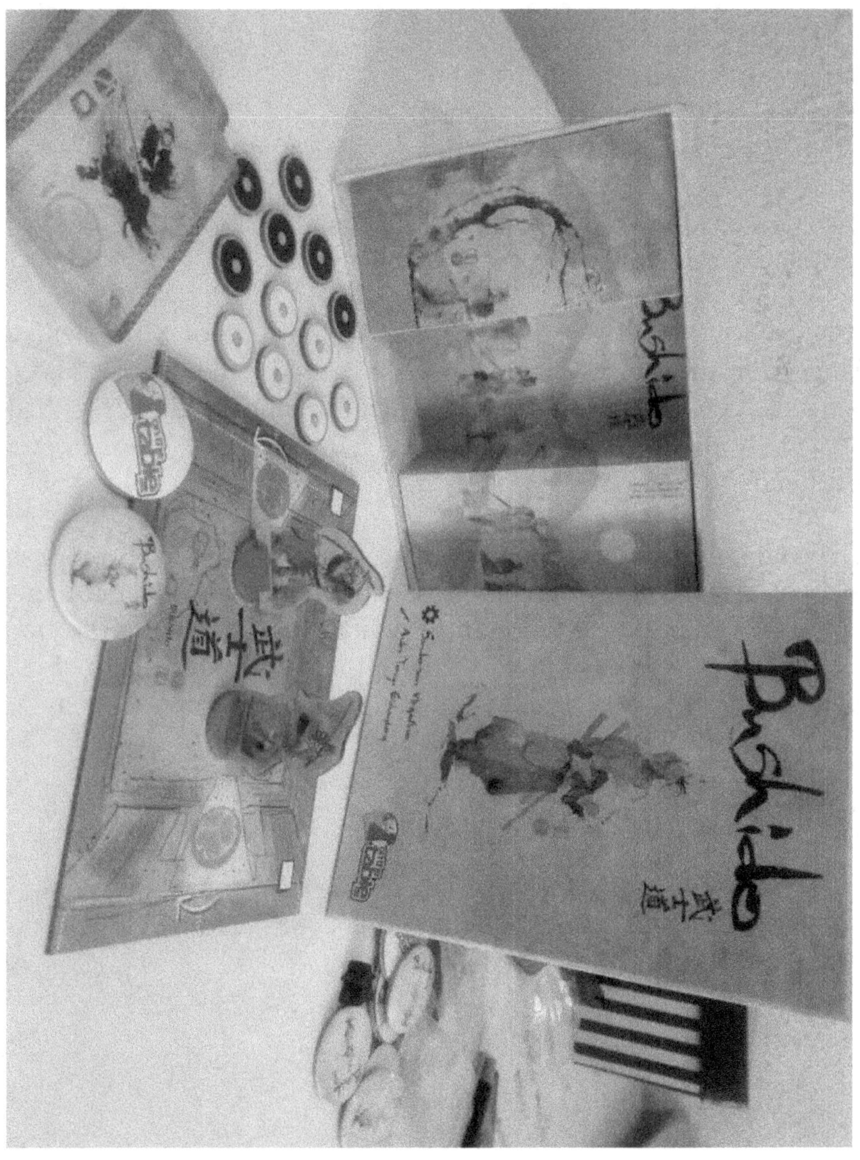

Cangaço
Released: 2020
Board, Card or other analog game
www.boardgamegeek.com/boardgame/233962/cangaco

By: Casa do Goblin and Bureau de Juegos
Mesquita – RJ, Brazil

"Cangaço is a card game that returns to the time of the Brazilian cangaço, a movement characterized as social banditry that lasted between the last decades of the nineteenth century and the first half of the twentieth century, through the Brazilian Northeastern backlands.

The goal is to become the new "King of the cangaço", to accomplish this you´ll have to set up camps, prepare ambushes, join gunfights and gather 'cabras' who fight for the honor of their captain. Braveing the night of the sertão with the light of the lamp and the help of the 'coiteiros' you´ll have to survive many hardships on your way to victory."

Press:

https://medium.com/@sanvirgolino/2%C2%BA-concurso-game-of-boards-prot%C3%B3tipos-em-jogo-8ee68a2da2d6

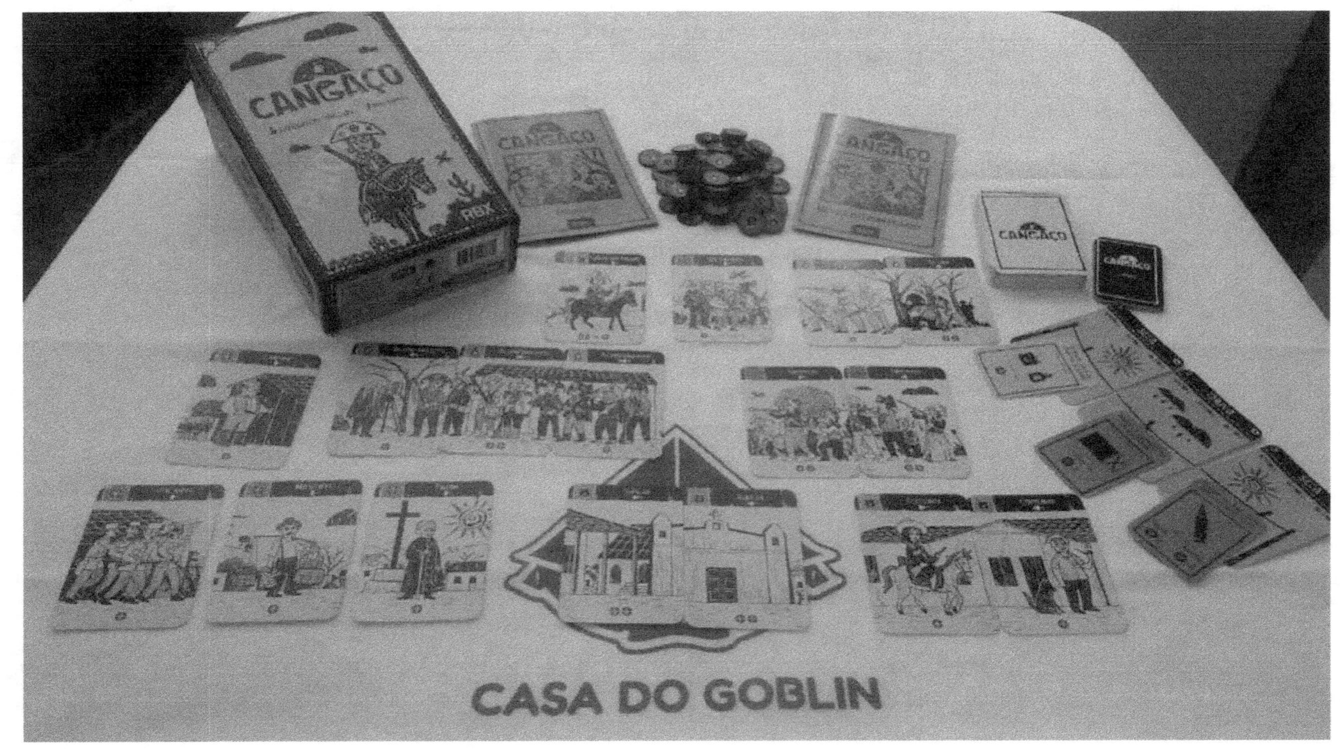
CANGAÇO
RBX
CASA DO GOBLIN

Earth Cipher

Released: 2021
Mobile: Android, Mobile: iOS
www.earthcipher.com

By: MediaBreeze Multimedia (Nmuta Jones)
Dar Es Salaam, Tanzania

Earth Cipher is a game about global economic justice. It uses the environment as a lens to explore that topic but in a way that is lighthearted and fun, for all ages.

You play that game alternating between human and animal player characters that are working together to reduce the carbon footprint of the human. There's a symbiotic relationship between these pairs and they learn to help each other. The first level is in Tanzania. There are a number of mischievous agents who are doing things to prevent you from reducing your carbon footprint in your area. You alternate between a human character and a Black Rhino who each can do things to manipulate the game world in a way that will reduce the individual carbon footprint of the human player.

The game has an open format where after getting started in the game, you can play any level, and the various levels of the game are located across several continents. There are levels in Sri Lanka, Mongolia, South America, Alaska, and various locations where endangered species exist.

One of the themes of the game is that due to the mounting effects and future projections of climate change, all of us are effectively endangered species on this Earth.

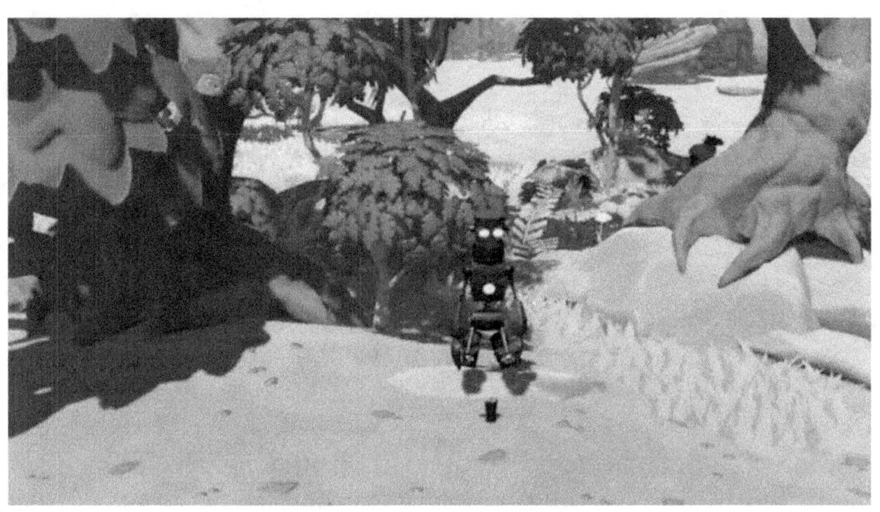

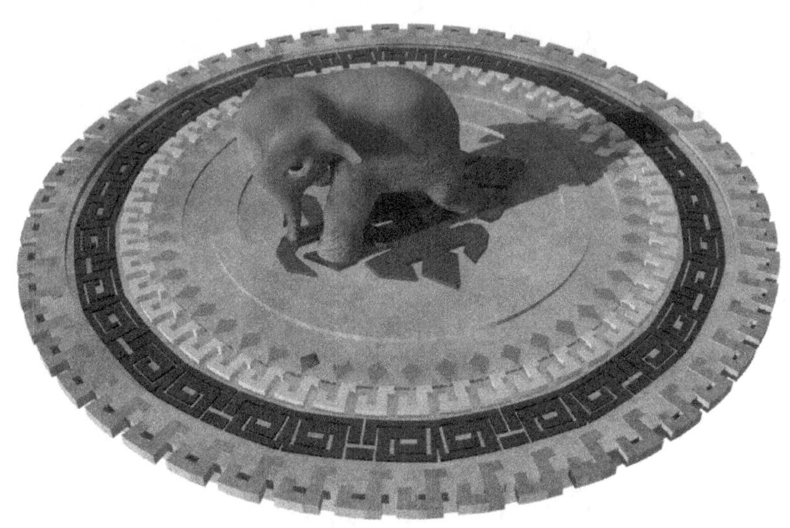

Election Day: The Game
Released: 2016
Board, Card or other analog game
www.facebook.com/Electiondaygame

By: Clay Street Marketing, LLC.
Washington, DC

Election Day: The game, is a dice-based turn game that allows between 2-4 players. The approximate play time is between 30-45minutes.

The objective if the game is to build up a campaign, using your campaign bus, by landing on and acquiring things you need like Office Space, Petition Signatures, and Fundraisers. Once that happens you get to put your candidate on the polling map, then candidates can move forward by rolling the political die and pulling the corresponding card, Conventional Wisdom cards move you forward and Scandal cards move you back. If a player rolls ""Political Play"" they can choose a conventional wisdom card for themselves or a scandal card for their opponent.

The first player to make it to the victory circle wins the game.

Notable Press:

WUSA9 Channel 9, Washington, DC (CBS Affiliate):

Great Day: https://www.youtube.com/watch?v=vFgMer6SNxU

https://www.youtube.com/watch?v=pjcp1fTN_x4

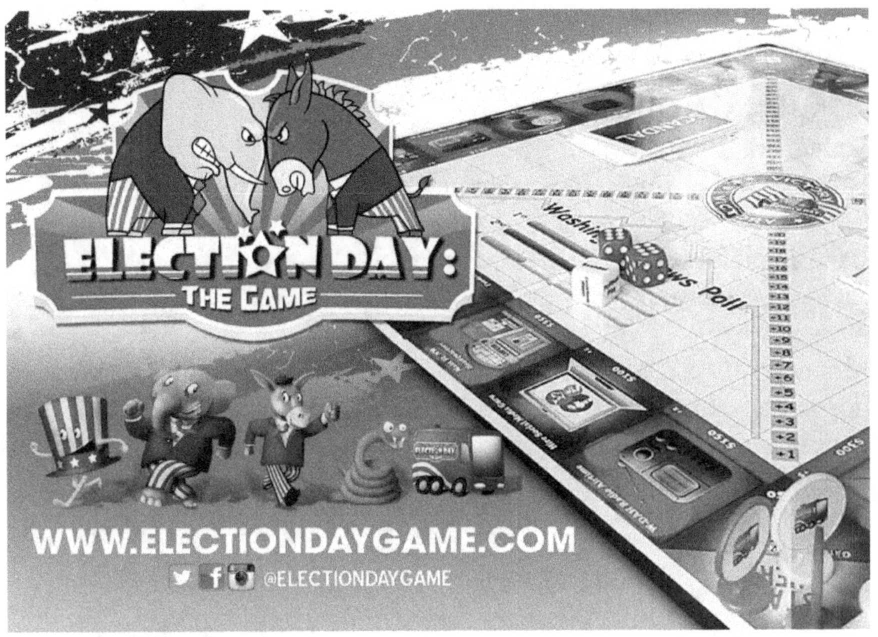
ELECTION DAY:
THE GAME
WWW.ELECTIONDAYGAME.COM
@ELECTIONDAYGAME

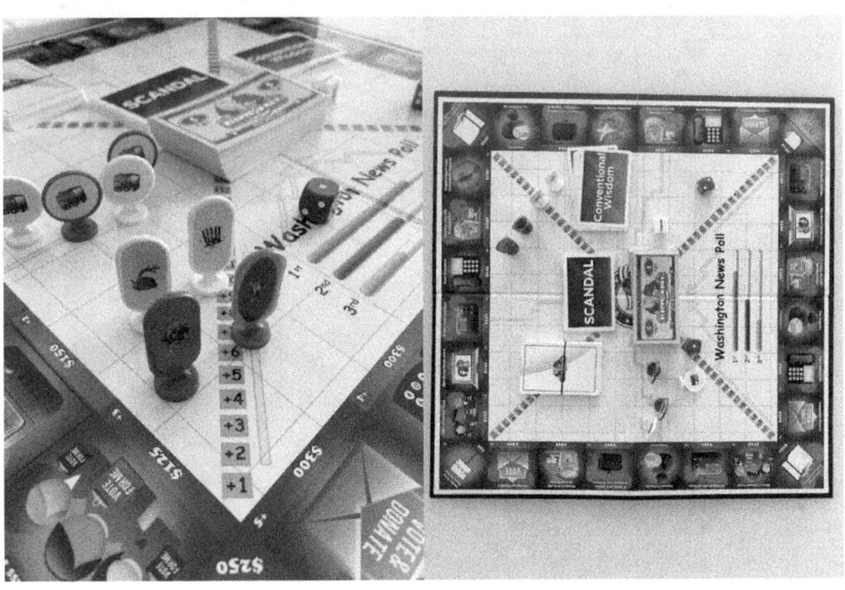
Conventional Wisdom
SCANDAL
Washington News Poll

FiQuestions

Released: 2020
Board, Card or other analog game

By: Financial IQ, LLC
Jackson, Misssippi

Financial IQ creates and provides financial products and services to normalize the discussion of finances with hopes to break generational curses and increase the financial intelligence of individuals by providing resources to help individuals understand the psychological factors that influence the thoughts and behaviors regarding finances

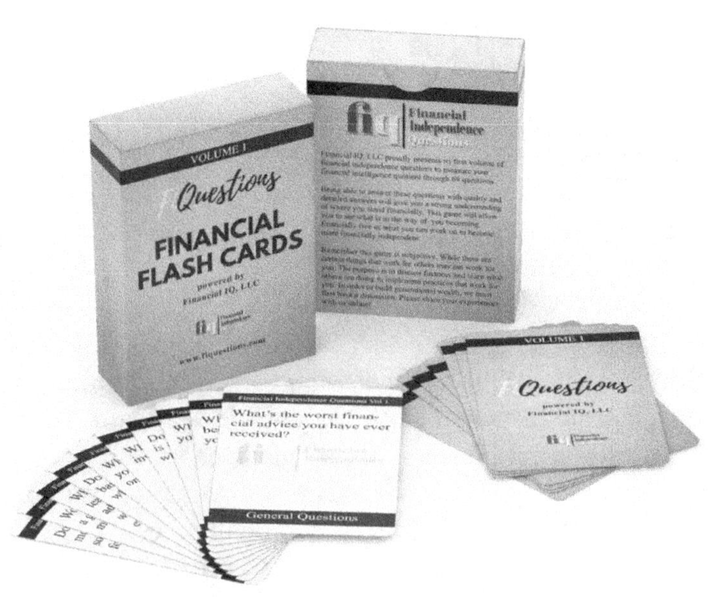

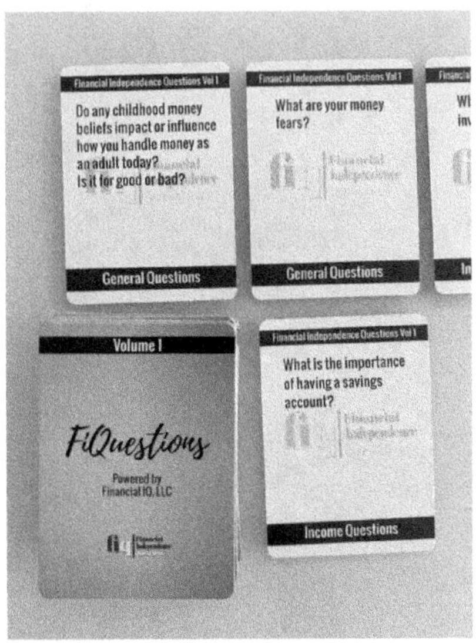

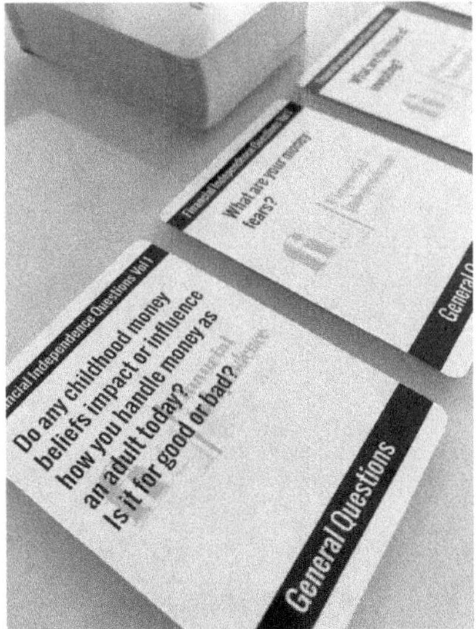

Galactic Bar Fight
Released: 2021
Oculus Quest
www.weirdkidstudios.com

By: Weird Kid Studios (Jonathan Jennings)
Los Angeles , California

Galactic Bar Fight is an arcade action game that positions players as an explorer on the edge of the galaxy. As they fight their way through various planets and environments in search of a drink . The game features blades, blasters, and explosives as you fight swathes of angry aliens and enemies focused on your destruction while utilizing powerups during intense timed challenges.

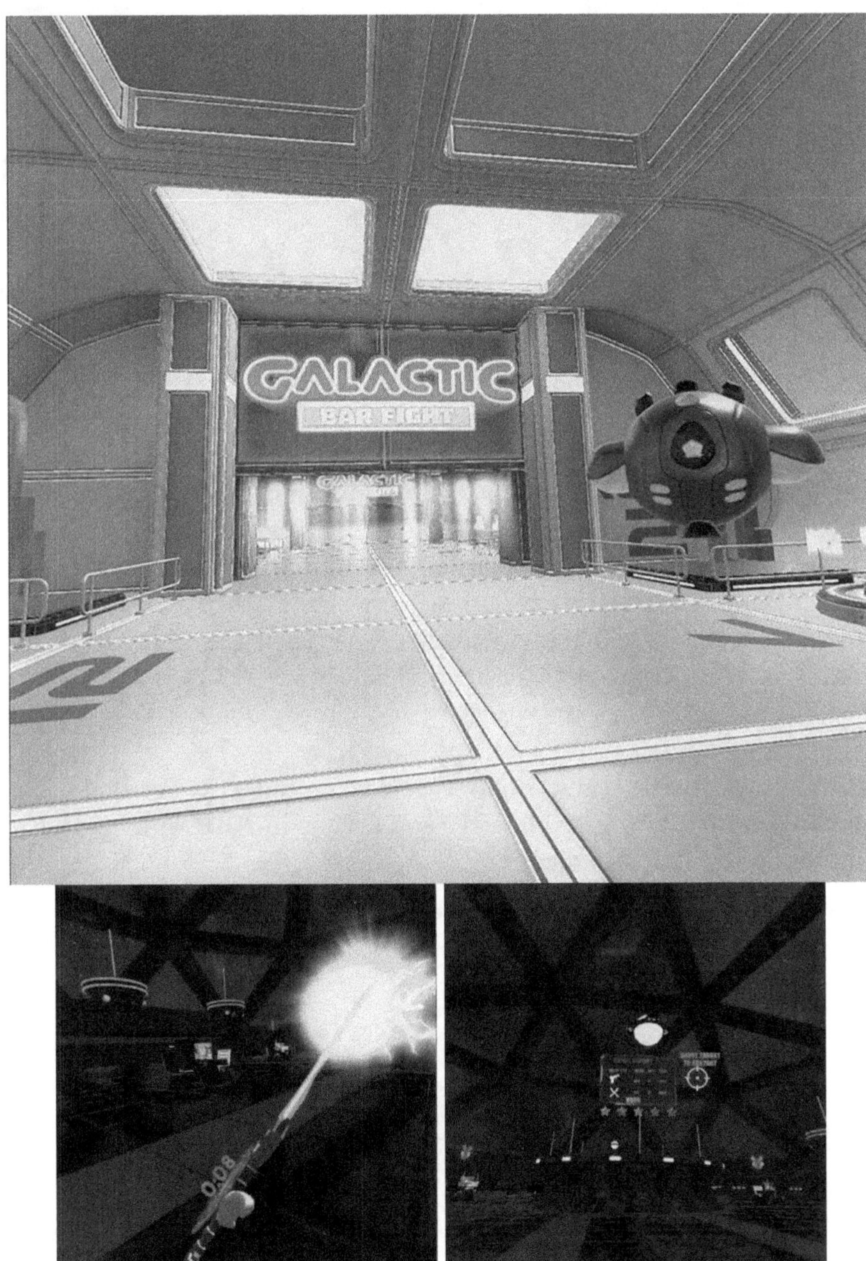
GALACTIC
BAR FIGHT
GALACTIC

Healer

Released: 2010 / 2019
Windows PC and HTML 5
Criticalgameplay.com/healer.html

By: Critical Gameplay (Lindsay Grace)
Oxford, Ohio / Miami, Florida

Instead of shooting characters, players must heal victims of historical massacres. The player can reverse death, by pulling bullets from the victims. The soldiers that committed these massacres are still lurking, so the player must work to keep the recently revived alive. The player can put themselves between the bullet and the target or strategize to reverse the tragedy.

The game depicts the Nanking Massacre, the largest historical atrocity whose fact and fiction were continuously debated. The original game was created in 2010 and redone in 2019 with upgraded hardware and performance.

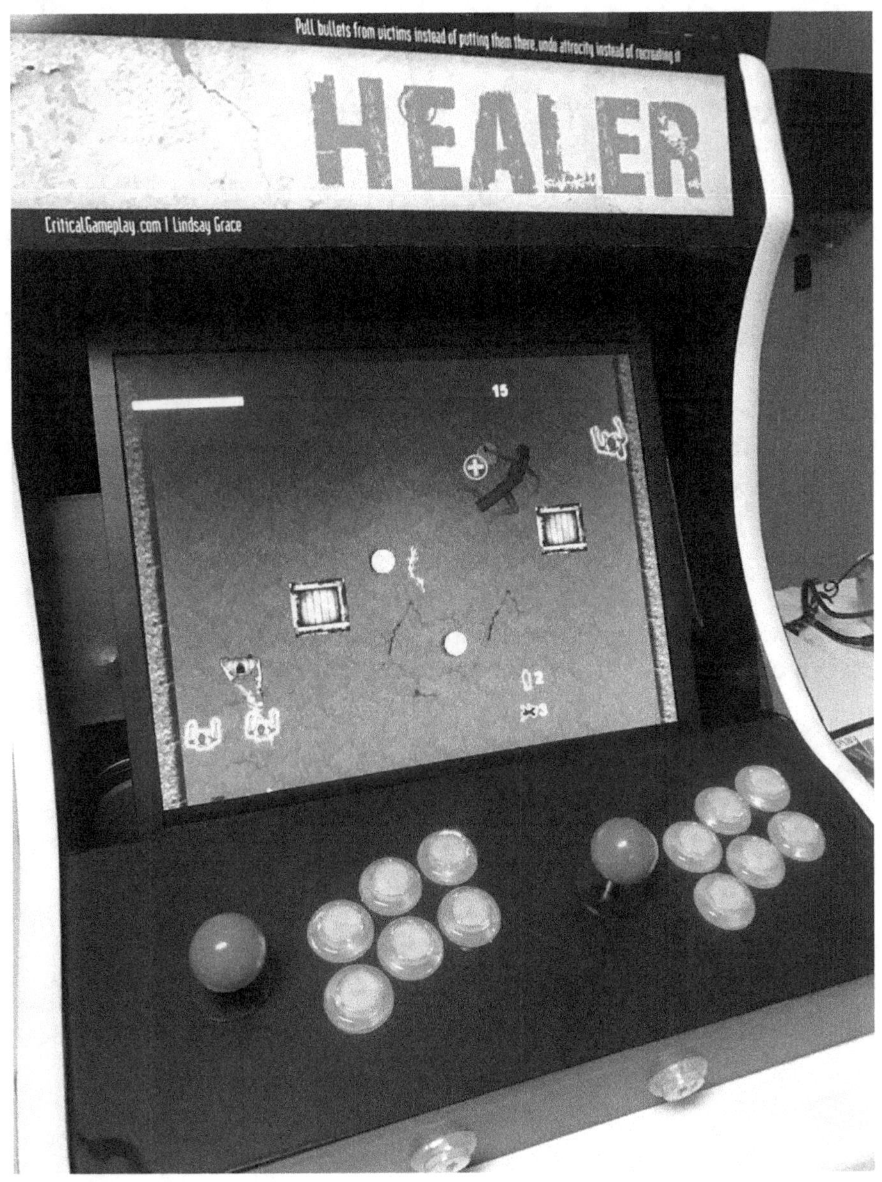
Pull bullets from victims instead of putting them there, undo atrocity instead of recreating it
HEALER
CriticalGameplay.com | Lindsay Grace
15

Home R Where The Heart Is
Released: 2019
Mac OS, Android, iOS, Windows 7, Windows 8, HTML 5
www.glorioustrainwrecks.com/node/11420

By: everythingstaken(Blake Andrews)
New York/New Jersey

The interaction is simple, mash space or touch the screen in order to make the home disappear and reappear. Each time it reappears a group of black Simpsons, furniture, and other environmental elements. fall into the home. When it disappears, the Simpsons and other objects fall. If the player rapidly switches the house off and on the game becomes a cacophony of animation and sound effects. If you do not do anything for a while you can see birds fly around the screen chirping and can look at procedurally placed cloud homes.

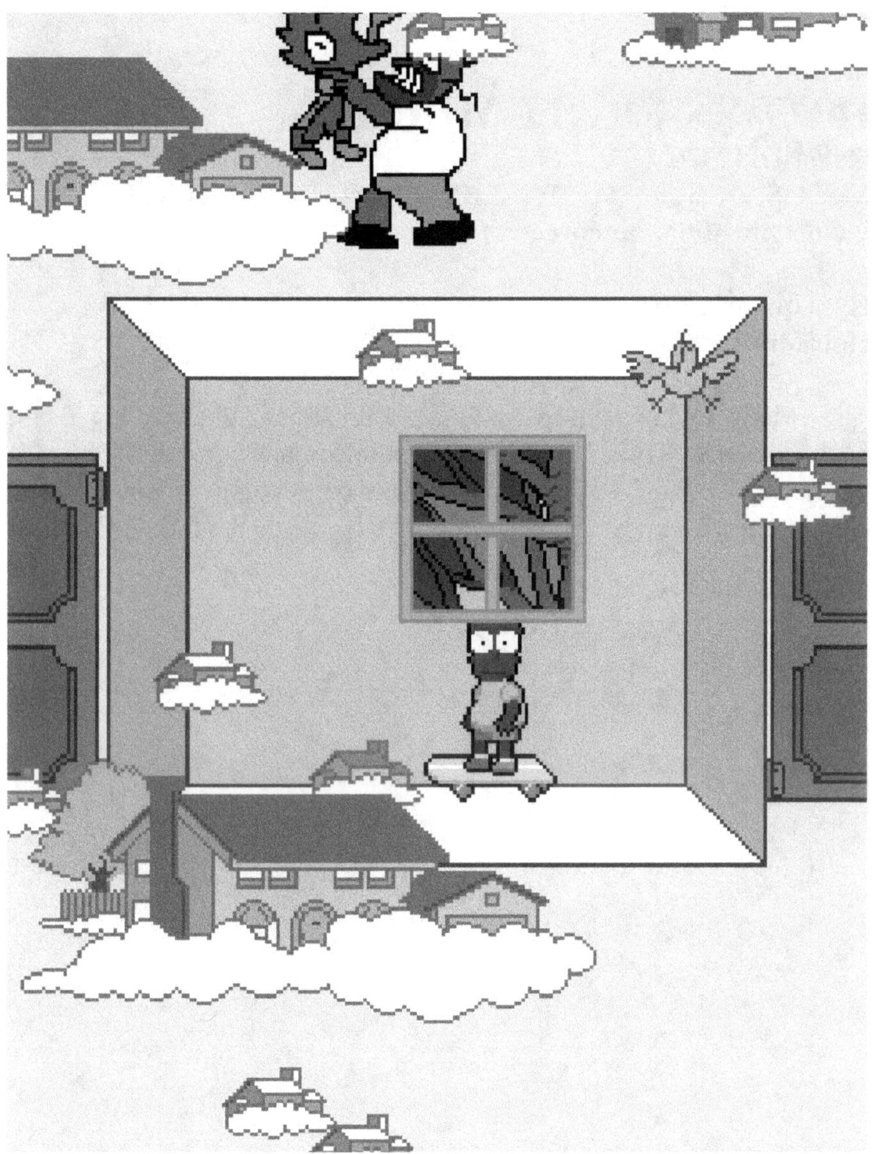

HTOWN FIGHT MINNIES

Released: 2020
Mac OS, Android, iOS, Windows XP, VISTA, or 7, Windows 8
www.htownfightminnies.com

By: Urban Tek CGI
Houston, Texas

The video game of hiphop combined with street fighter and Def Jam Fight for New York. Listen to your favorite artist music while you pounce on your OP. Win battles and earn coins to unlock new characters. Or play story mode and try to become the KING OF THE SOUTH.

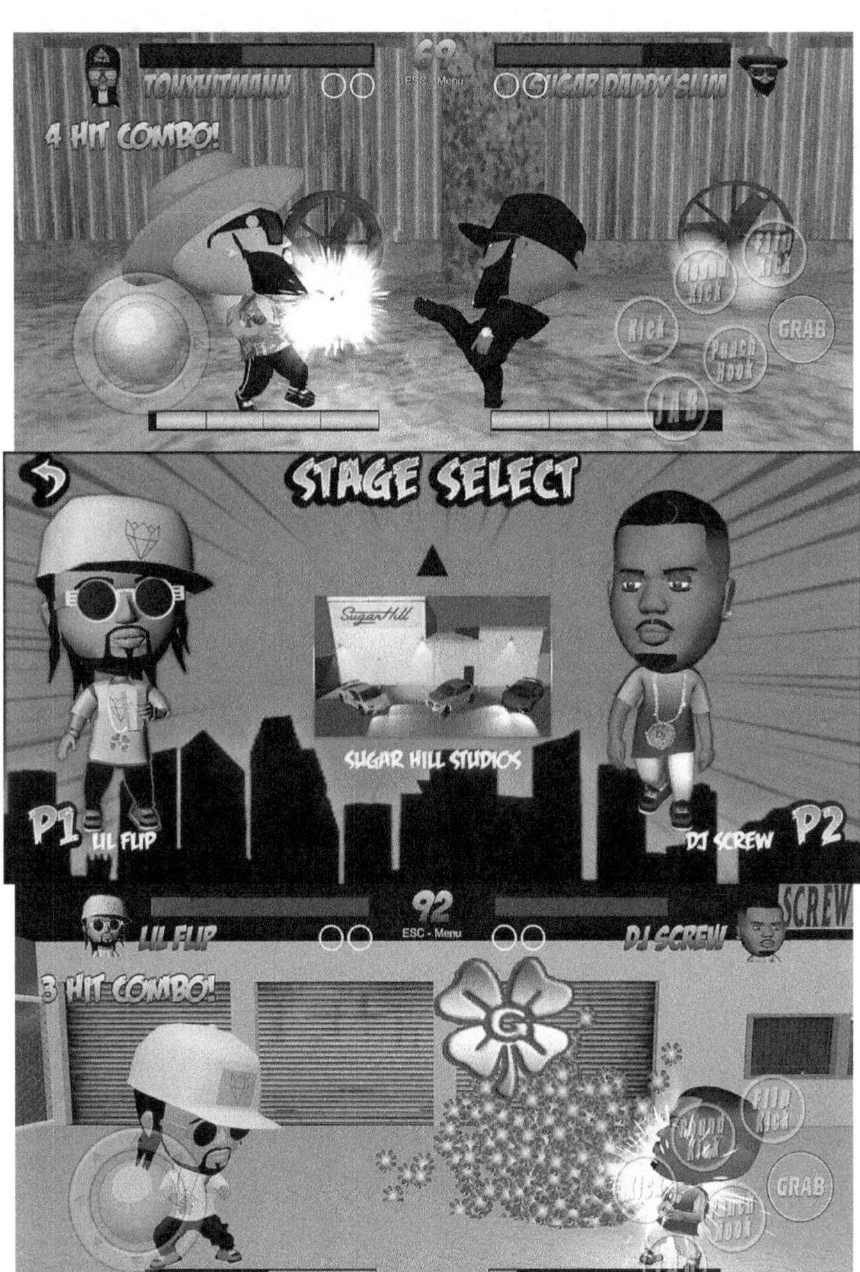

TONYHITMANN
SUGAR DADDY SLIM
4 HIT COMBO!
ESC - Menu
ROUND KICK
FLIP KICK
KICK
GRAB
PUNCH HOOK
JAB
STAGE SELECT
Sugar Hill
SUGAR HILL STUDIOS
P1 LIL FLIP
DJ SCREW P2
LIL FLIP
DJ SCREW
ESC - Menu
3 HIT COMBO!
SCREW
G
ROUND KICK
FLIP KICK
GRAB
PUNCH HOOK
JAB

Inequality-opoly: The Board Game of Structural Racism and Sexism in America

Released: 2016
Board game, Mac OS, Windows XP, VISTA, or 7, Windows 8
www.inequalityopoly.com

By: Perry Clemons
New York, New York

Inequality-opoly: The Board Game of Structural Racism and Sexism in America is an educational property trading game that transforms recent national studies into a perspective taking experience. In this game, as in the real world, certain players enjoy privileges based on their perceived identity while others face obstacles to building and sustaining wealth. The Mission of Inequality-opoly is to spread awareness and advance discourse about how structural racism and sexism affect the accumulation and sustaining of wealth in America

Press:

Forbes, July 29, 2020:
        http://bit.ly/ineqforbes

Speaking of Racism:
        http://bit.ly/sorineq

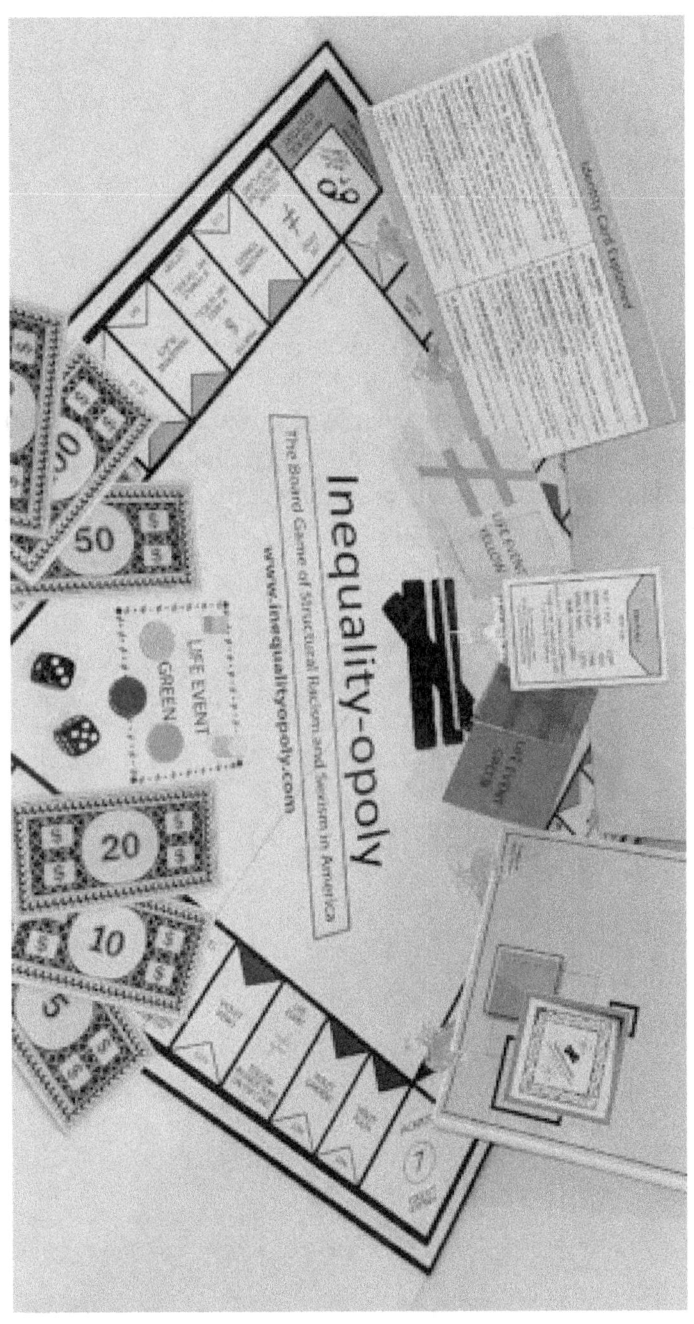
Inequality-opoly
The Board Game of Structural Racism and Sexism in America
www.inequalityopoly.com
LIFE EVENT
GREEN
50
20
10
5

Karaoke Kards

Released: 2020
Board, Card or other analog game
Karaokekards.com

By: Katrina Mickle
Charlotte, NC

This game is designed to make everyone feel like a Superstar. Not knowing which song you will have to sing makes karaoke spontaneous. The cards will also help guide those who are not sure which song they want to sing. You will be challenged to sing a song which falls in the category listed on the card. There are also special cards in the deck to shake things up.

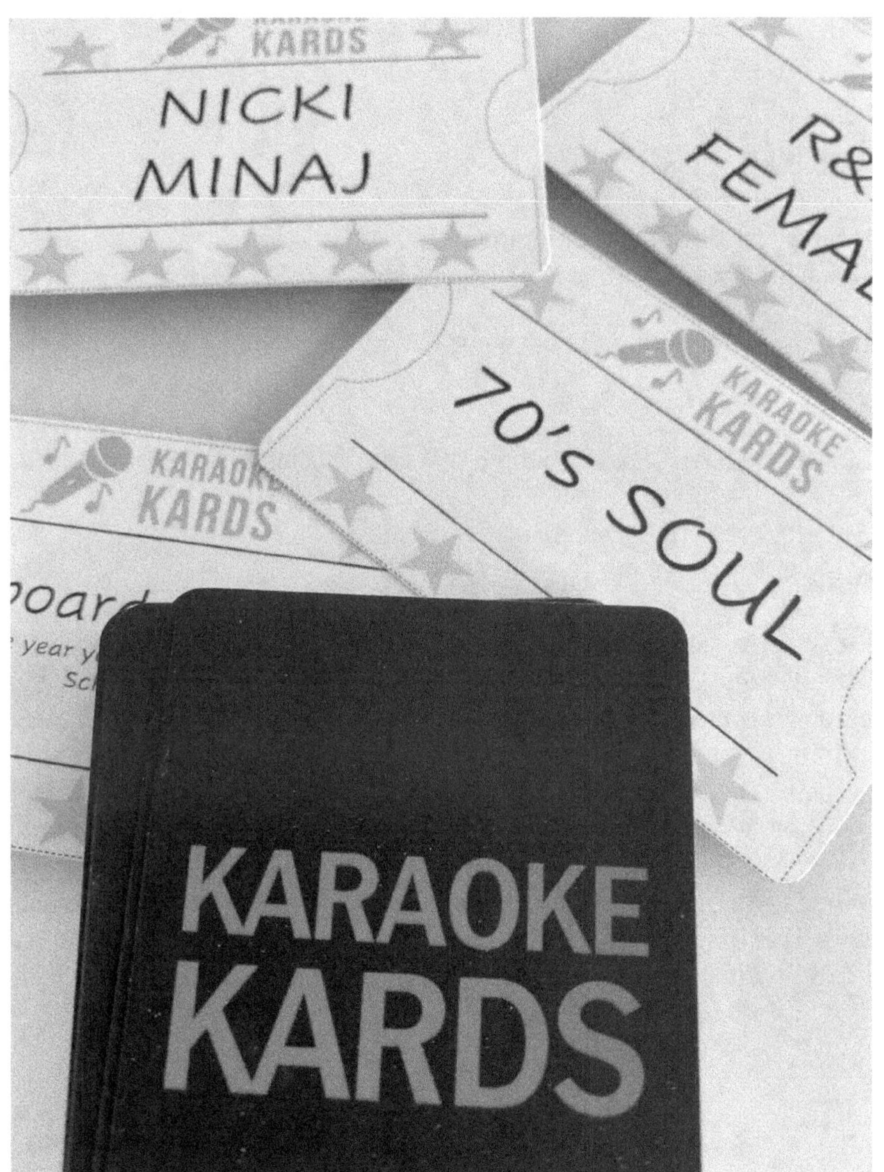
KARAOKE
KARDS
NICKI
MINAJ
R&
FEMA
70's SOUL
KARAOKE
KARDS
KARAOKE
KARDS
KARAOKE
KARDS

La Muerte

Released: 2018
Board, Card or other analog game
www.ludopedia.com.br/jogo/la-muerte

By: Casa do Goblin e Sherlock SA
Mesquita / RJ

La Muerte has a job: kill people that has finished their time on Earth.

But not everyone wants to die. Some people try to run. But La Muerte don't give up.

La Muerte starts the game with Wrath value 1. Every card has a ""Run"" and ""Wrath"" values. In your turn, you can play until 3 cards and sum the Run value to be equal or greater than La Muerte's Wrath. If you run, La Muerte get's more anger and its Wrath value is increased, according with the played cards. If you can't, you died. As ghost, you only increment La Muerte's Wrath, and helps it to kill!

When only one player is alive, he/she has one turn to stay alive and win! But if La Muerte, with the ghosts' help, kills this last player, nobody wins, except La Muerte!!"

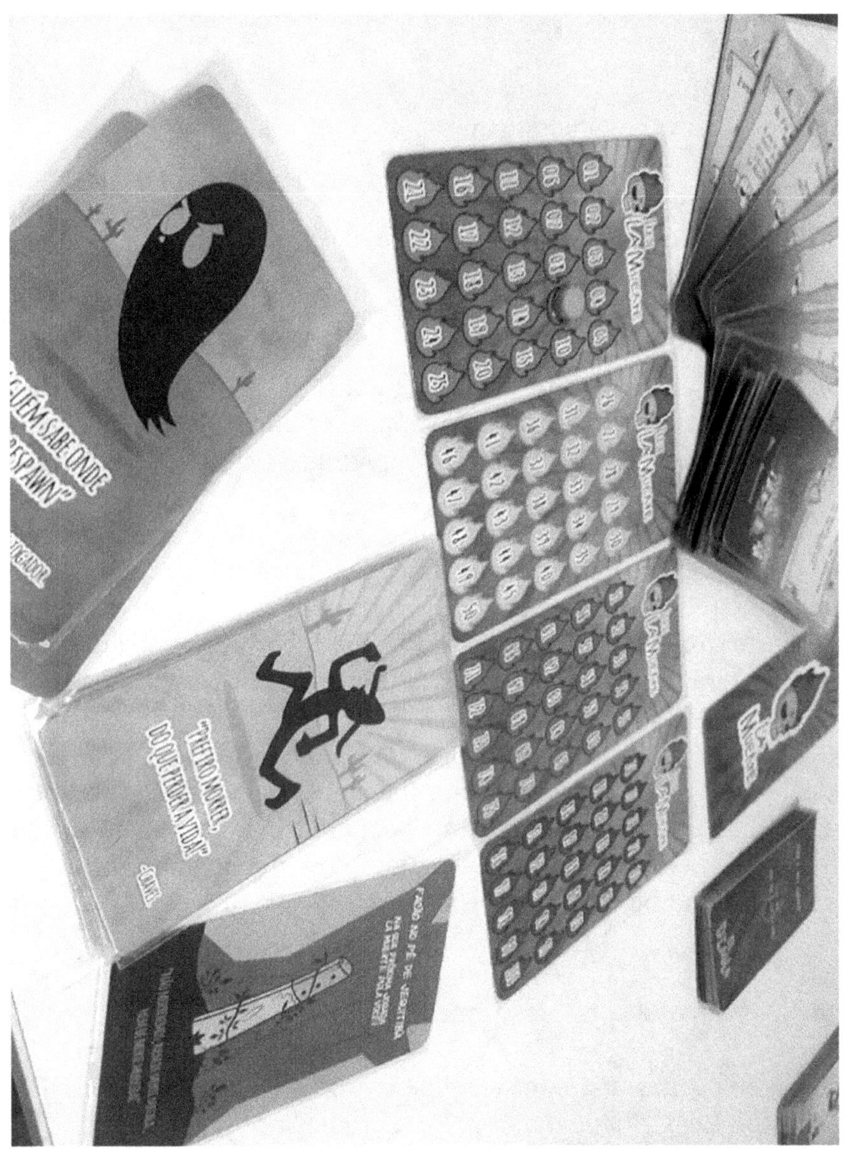

Objectif

Released: 2012
Board, Card or other analog game
prettydarke.cool/portfolio/objectif/

By: A.M. Darke
Los Angeles, California

In 2011 Psychology Today posted an article entitled "Why are Black Women Less Attractive than Other Races?" In response, I created the game Objectif, forcing players to confront how personal preferences are informed by white supremacist and colorist beauty standards.

Each round one player acts as the judge, while other players compete to place the most attractive card. In Objectif, the judge must explain their reason for choosing one card over the others, giving players an opportunity to influence, argue, and persuade their way to victory.

The game consists of illustrations of Black women, and each character has a doppelgänger with the same facial features but the pigment has changed. When two doppelgängers are played in the same round, every player must consider how pigmentation impacts their understanding of attractiveness.

Press:
Game Developer Magazine, September 2017:

https://www.gamasutra.com/view/news/305183/Frog_Fractions_2_
A_Normal_Lost_Phone_among_2017_IndieCade_nominees.php

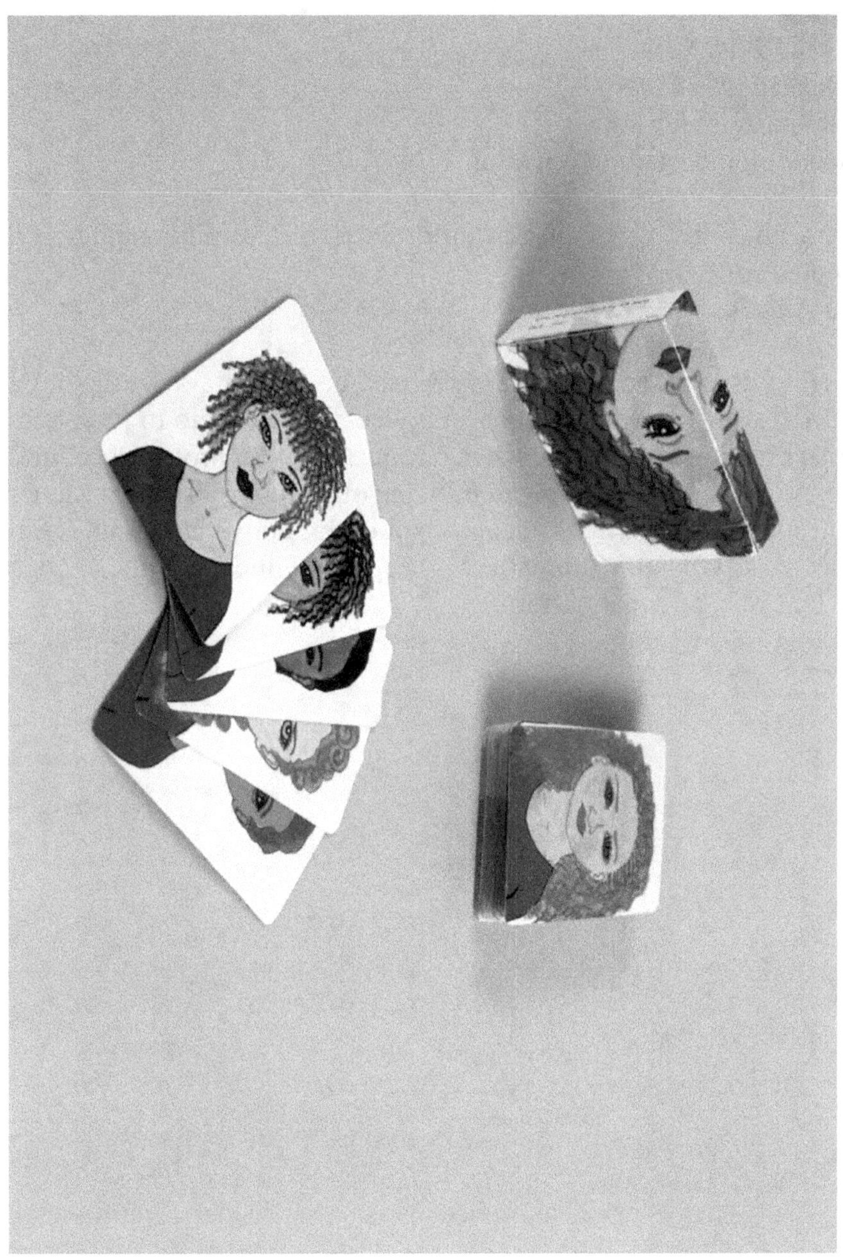

Operator

Released: 2020
Mac OS, Windows 8
https://jpjupiter.itch.io/operator

By: University of Southern California team (Jasmine Jupiter and Cloud Tian)
Los Angeles, CA

Operator is an interactive audio-drama where the player embodies a journalist, Imani, who must use a police-scanner radio to monitor a protest and protect her sister, Tema, as the protest becomes dangerous. It is a game inspired by the ongoing Black Lives Matter protests and the struggle against police brutality. Utilizing a full voice cast, Operator dramatizes sweeping political events through the lens of a personal narrative.

Black Game Studies

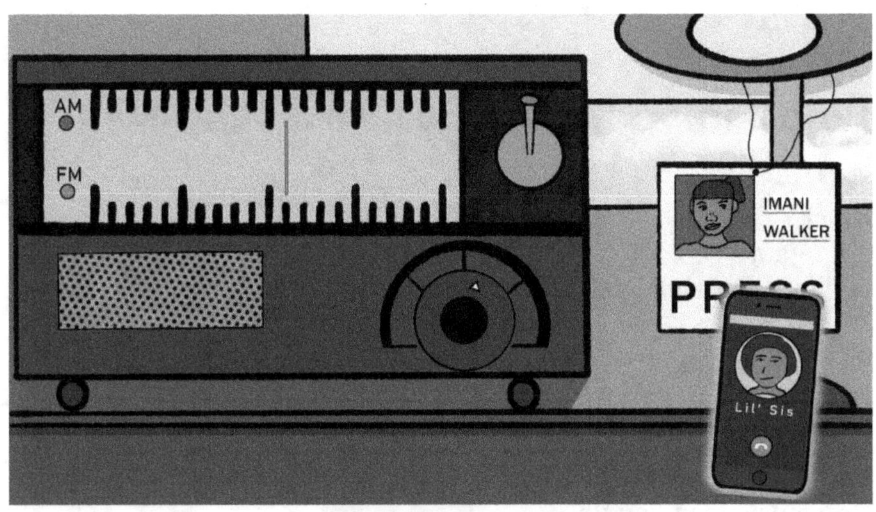

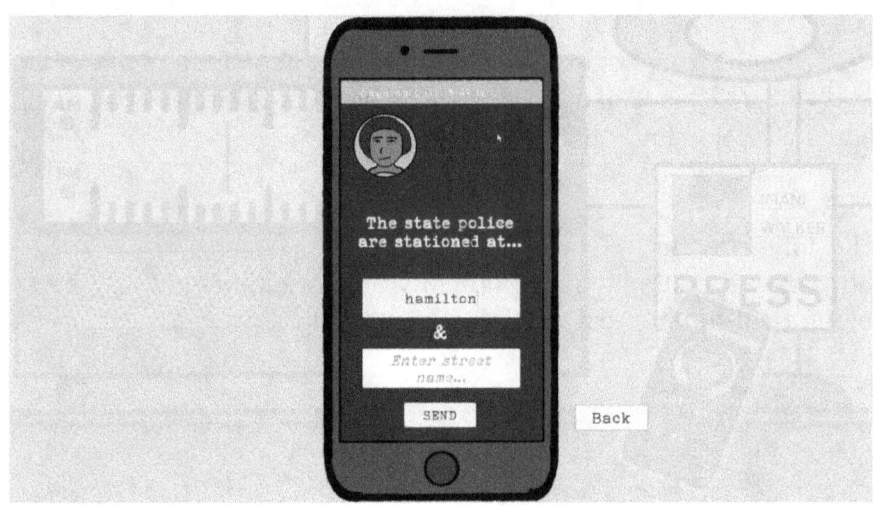

Pull Your Card Music Trivia: Hip Hop Edition

Released: 2017
Card game
pullyourcardtrivia.com

By: Pull Your Card
Enfield, CT

We all have that one friend who thinks they know more about Hip Hop music than you do 🙄

Prove them wrong and show that your trivia knowledge is superior. With the assistance of a few Game Changer cards, protect your hand and don't let them Pull Your Card!

Press:
Hartford Courant
https://www.courant.com/community/bloomfield/hc-news-bloomfield-hip-hop-trivia-20180425-story.html

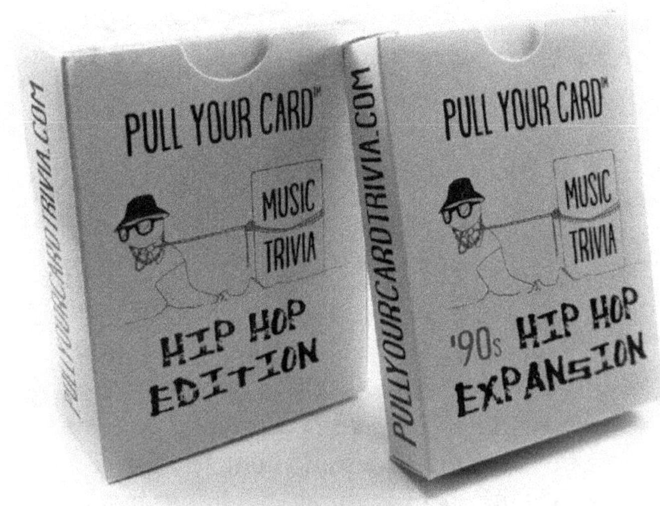
PULL YOUR CARD™
MUSIC TRIVIA
HIP HOP EDITION
PULLYOURCARDTRIVIA.COM
PULL YOUR CARD™
MUSIC TRIVIA
'90s HIP HOP EXPANSION
PULLYOURCARDTRIVIA.COM
PULLYOURCARDTRIVIA.COM

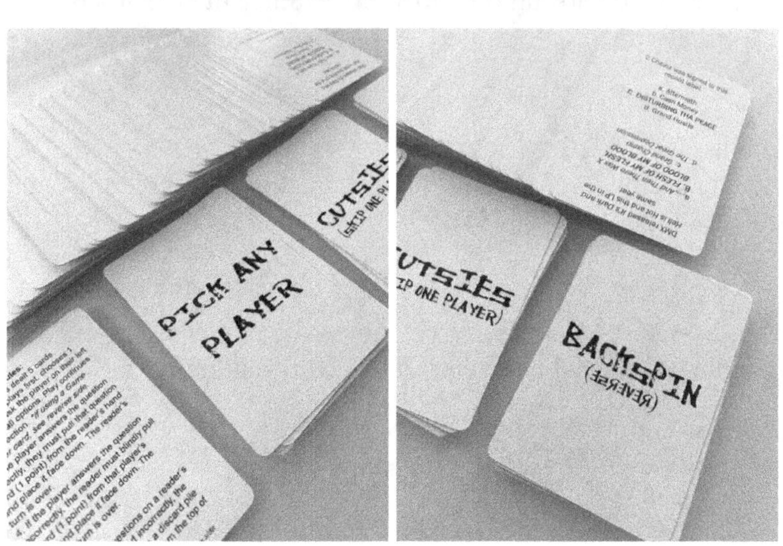
PICK ANY PLAYER
CUTSIES (SKIP ONE PLAYER)
CUTSIES (SKIP ONE PLAYER)
BACKSPIN (REVERSE)

Rap Godz

Released: 2020
Board game
https://www.boardgamebrothas.com/rap-godz

By: Board Game Brothas
New Orleans, LA

RAP GODZ is a modern board game that puts you in the role of an up and coming hip-hop artist on your path to greatness.

The gameplay is a mix of strategy and storytelling as you play cards that represent events in your emcee's career and life. Along the way you will have to earn money, build up your street cred, and improve your rap skillz. Starting beef with players might put you on top but can also knock you out when you least expect it.

Prove you are the ultimate Rap God by taking over cities, hitting career goals, and earning the most record sales plaques by the end of your third album.

Press:
Gizmodo, June 2020
https://io9.gizmodo.com/rap-godz-co-creator-shares-why-he-made-one-of-the-indus-1844064580

Dicebreaker
https://www.dicebreaker.com/categories/board-game/opinion/black-board-games-future-of-tabletop

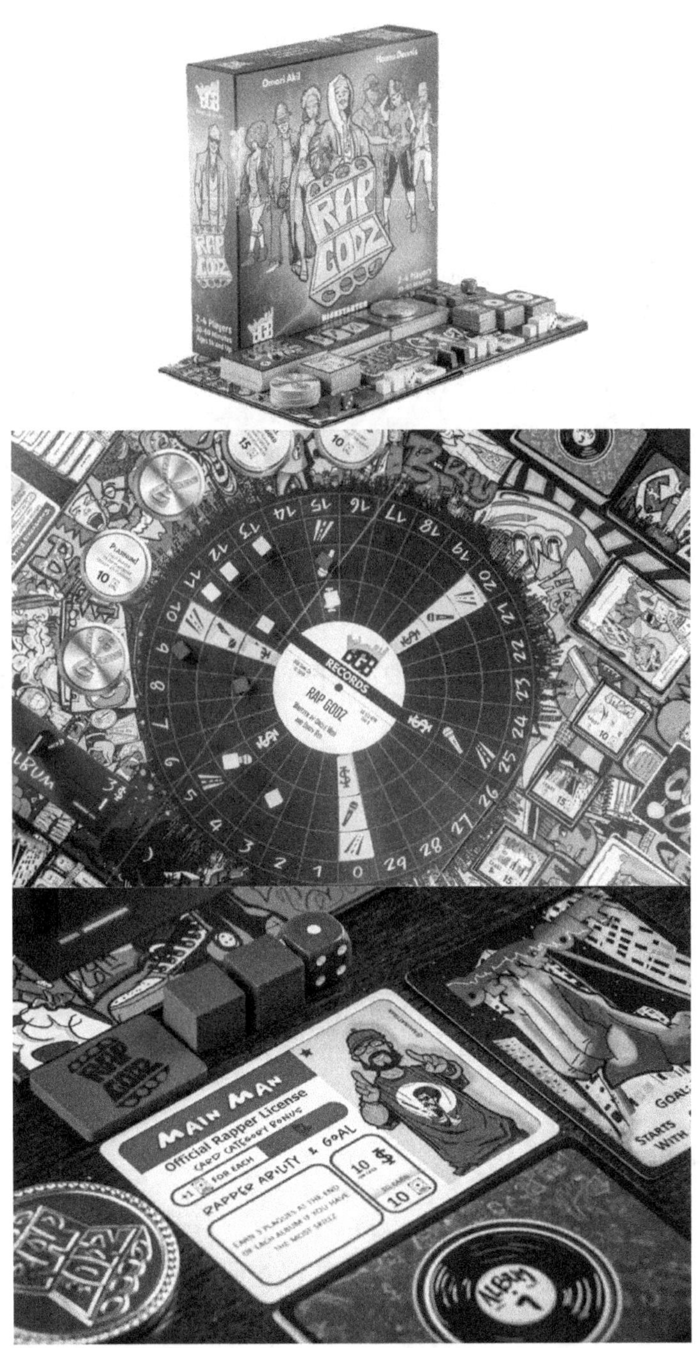

Rite in Rolls
Released: 2020
Analog game via Zoom

By: illest Preacha & Rmablin Intelluct
Montréal, Canada

Objective: Players collaborate on writing up a poetic piece.

Needed: Dice (Virtual or Real), Word Document

Player Mode: Versus or team (Maximum 4 per team; maximum 4 teams)

Rules
• Dice is throw to determine first player. Highest number is first player
• Player throws dice. Player is to write a poem with number of lines being number from dice.

• In versus mode, each player has 30 seconds per turn. In team mode, each team has 1 minute per turn.

• End of game: for versus mode, a minimum of 4 turns ends the game. For team mode, minimum of 2 rounds ends the game.

Points
• Completed Lines: 1 point per line in versus mode; 3 points per line in team mode
• Most Completed Lines: 5 bonus points per line in versus mode; 10 points per line in team mode.
• Incomplete Lines: deduct 2 points per line in versus mode; deduct 4 points per line in team mode.

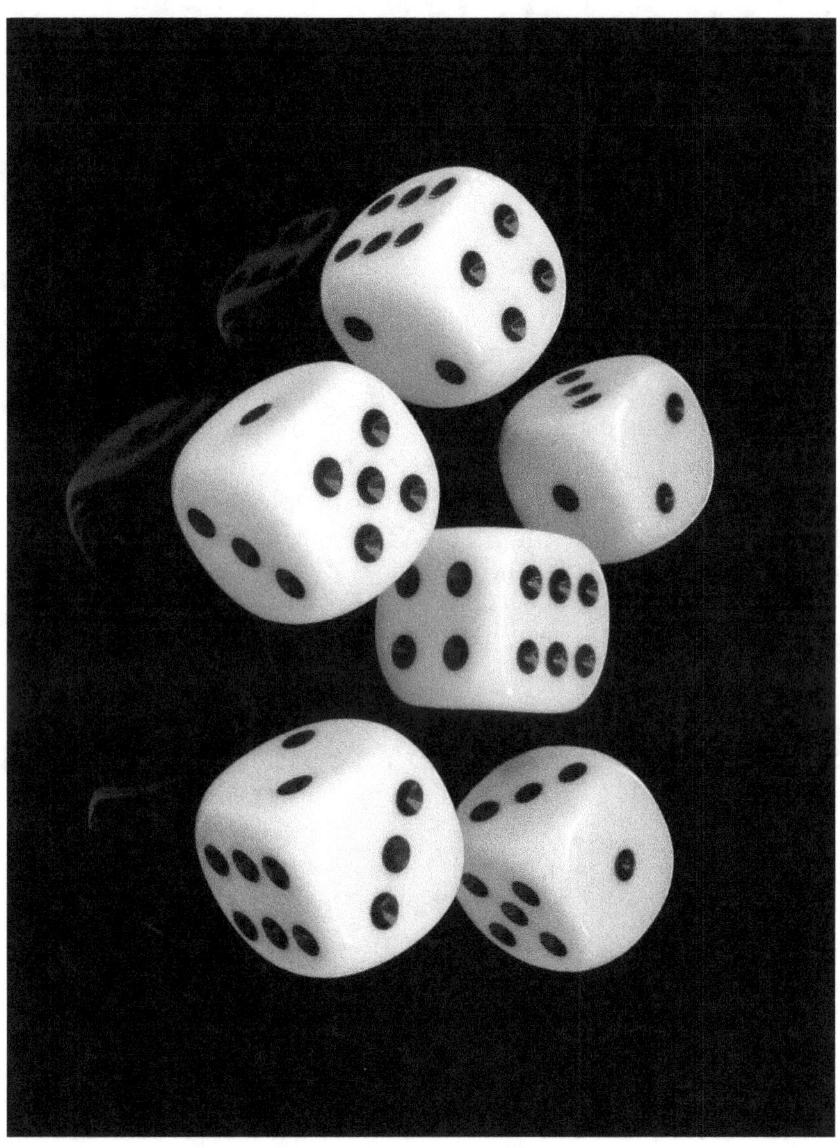

Run Die Run Again

Released: 2021
Console: Playstation, Xbox, or Wii, Windows 10
https://www.retroninja.com/about

By: RetroNinja Inc.
Orange County   , California

It is 2127 and the divide between the "haves" and "have-nots" has grown to astronomical proportions. To give the masses entertainment and hope of being elevated from their state of poverty, the governments of the world formed a "lottery meets Olympics", in the form of the contest called, "The Run". In The Run, athletes are selected to navigate virtual obstacle courses, filled with deadly hazards. The courses are so tough that people started calling the game, "Run, Die, Run Again" or "RDRA", for short. Eventually, The Run was renamed, to Run, Die, Run Again.

If a contestant can survive the increasingly difficult and varied courses, they win a coveted spot among "The Selected". The Selected are given food, shelter and never have to work again. In a world with very little light, RDRA and being "Selected" is like a blinding sun.

In Run Die Run Again, speed through stunning sci-fi obstacle courses; executing death-defying leaps, flips and dashes past deadly hazards and skirting certain-death, all with a ticking time-bomb strapped to your back! A precision platformer built for speed freaks who want their hardcore platformers in first-person.

Press:
https://vulgarknight.com/run-die-run-again/
https://linuxgameconsortium.com/run-die-run-again-precision-platformer-wants-you/

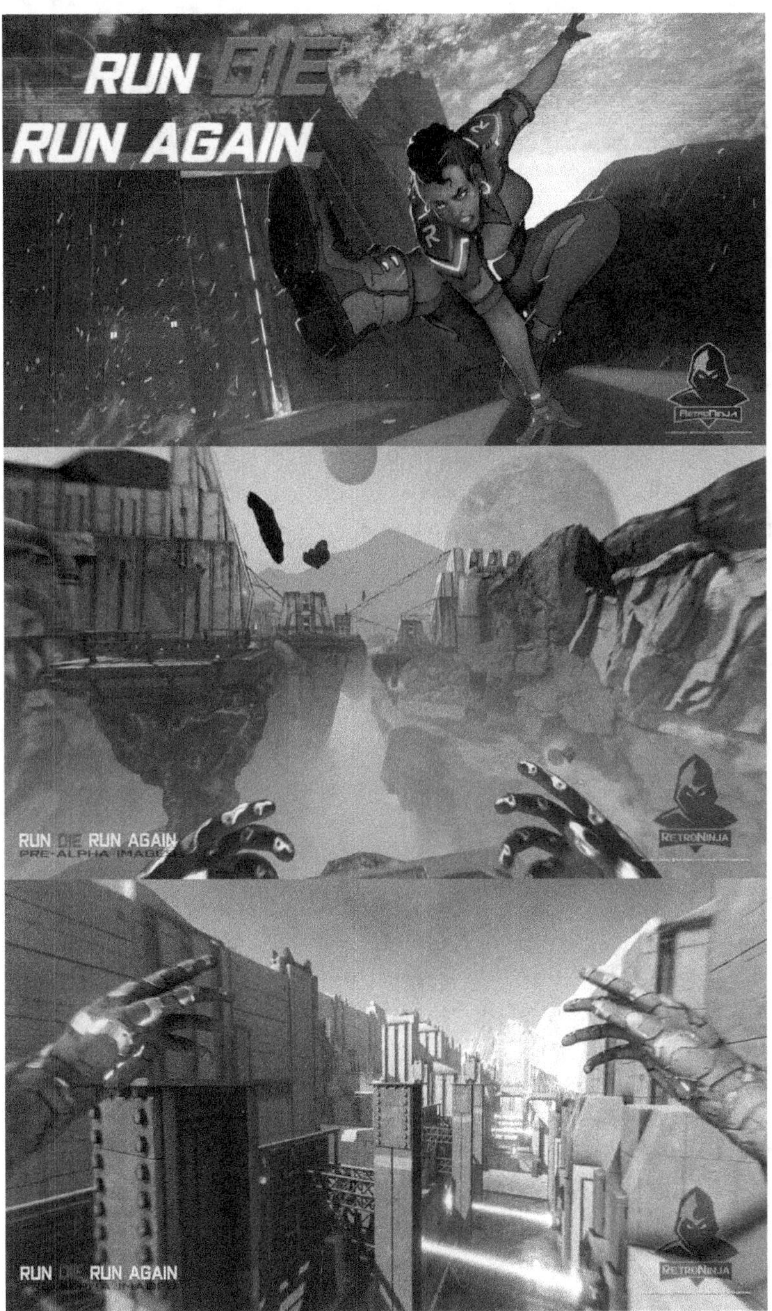
RUN DIE
RUN AGAIN
RetroNinja
RUN DIE RUN AGAIN
PRE-ALPHA IMAGES
RetroNinja
RUN DIE RUN AGAIN
RetroNinja

SPILL IT Card Game
Released: 2019
Board, Card or other analog game, Virtual gathering platforms: zoom, google meets, duo, etc
www.spillitcardgame.com

By: SPILL IT Card Game
Charlotte, North Carolina

Fine! We'll Spill It! - (The Origin Story)
SPILL IT was born from a group of college friends who have enjoyed a glass of wine (or two) and great conversation. Small conversations and a few glasses later led to funny and wildly passionate debates, then BOOM wine night became a huge tradition for us! Friends were free to openly spill their unfiltered experiences and opinions. We've embarked on this business venture to create card games that challenge friends and family to speak their truth and ignite conversation to get to know each other better. But trust us, as the wine flows, the conversation can get heated so play at your own risk!

Our Vision
Spill It Card Game is a set of cards filled with thought-provoking conversation starters to be played with family and friends. We want everyone to engage in questions with raw unfiltered answers that sparks an open discussion for the group! (If you end up getting a little tipsy in the process, we want that too). The goal is to learn about the people around you by sharing experiences that range from goofy and embarrassing to innovative and romantic. Spill It Card Game is meant to be played in a judgement free zone as we want you to bear it all!

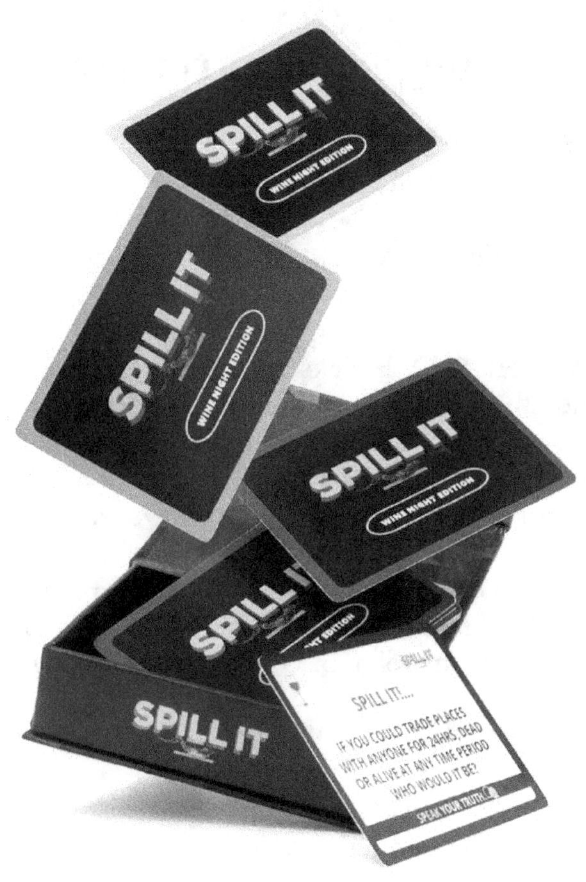
SPILL IT
WINE NIGHT EDITION
SPILL IT
WINE NIGHT EDITION
SPILL IT
WINE NIGHT EDITION
SPILL IT
SPILL IT
SPILL IT!...
IF YOU COULD TRADE PLACES
WITH ANYONE FOR 24HRS, DEAD
OR ALIVE AT ANY TIME PERIOD
WHO WOULD IT BE?
SPEAK YOUR TRUTH

Street Team: Reign of the Iron Dragon
Released: 2011
Windows XP, VISTA, or 7, Windows 8
https://almightystreetteam.net/

By: Street Team Studios
Atlanta, GA

STREET TEAM: THE GAME picks up where the acclaimed comic left off. It unites the champions from five different independent comics to face an adversary so cunning and dangerous that working together is their only hope. GRANDMASTER OGUUN and his clan of conquerors known as the Silver Lords have taken Bridgeport City by storm with a large-scale surprise attack!
Join TIGER, DODGER, STALKER, THE VIGILANTE and BLACKBIRD as they battle their way from Atlanta to Bridgeport City as you try and stop the reign of Oguun, the Iron Dragon!

Press:

https://afropunk.com/2015/03/feature-the-almighty-street-team-how-we-created-our-own-comic-bookvideo-game-studio/

https://ghettomanga.blogspot.com/2011/05/preview-almighty-street-team-comic-and.html"

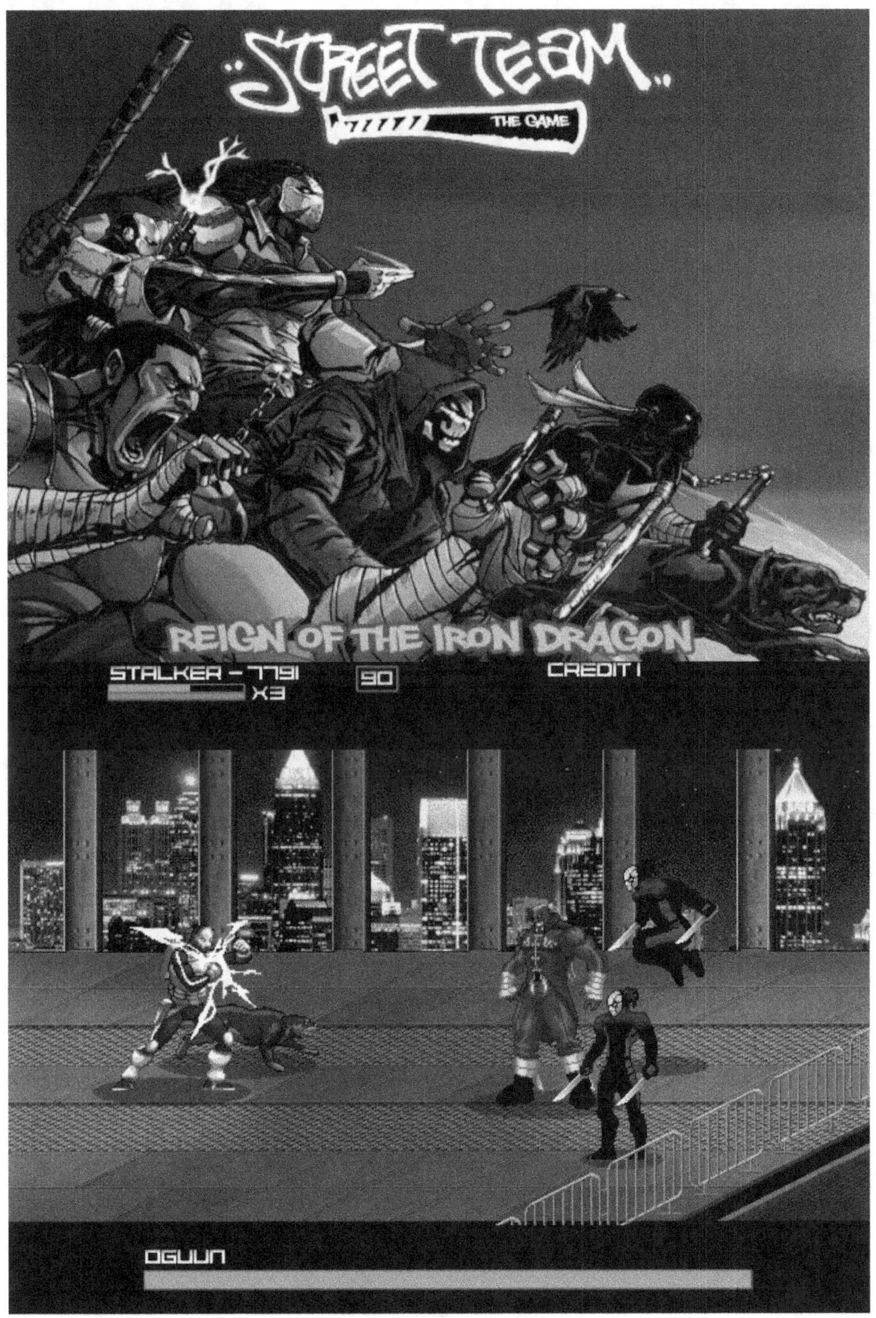
STREET TEAM
THE GAME
REIGN OF THE IRON DRAGON
STALKER - 7791
X3
90
CREDIT 1
OGUUN

Super High Dunk

Released: 2021
Windows XP, VISTA, or 7, Windows 8, Will be for PC, android and iPhone
https://youtu.be/xCUde6AoJnY

By: Eyedrinox Games
Rochester, New York

Growing up in the hood is tough. All we have is each other. That is until today! Kids from our hood have all started to go missing. They have been kidnapped by an evil clown with a vendetta against his past but is taking it out on us kids. They call him Nosy the clown. Nosy sent his creodont's out to lure children to him by placing hypnotizing TV's in their homes, to get them to follow his every command. They begin to transform into little purple creodonts and would reek chaos in the hood. Fortunately, for my 2 little brothers and I, we were not harmed but we had to do something about it. We set out to find our friends, even though we snuck out of the apartment - "mom's gonna kill us". We found out that the only way for us to save the hood is to beat them in an event called Super High Dunk. It is a mixed style sports event, championed for years by Nosy.

Legend has it, there was only one person good enough to beat him, but he lost to Nosy in the past and hasn't been seen sense. I went out to find if the legend was true and it was. I found him. His name was Pyro and he was living in a secluded area away from the public. I told him what was going on. He trained me and I trained my brothers and entered the event dressed as clowns to pay homage to Him. I had no clue that it was about to get so crazy. I found that the winner would be granted the power to rule the world for one year. Nosy somehow created shortcut portals to enter in and out of different areas that he too controls to make it impossible for there to ever be a new champion. We must defeat him in Super High Dunk in order to save the day, but it wont be easy, he has a kid protecting every portal that will stop you from winning by cheating. The more we seek, the more we find that there is something deeper to be found!

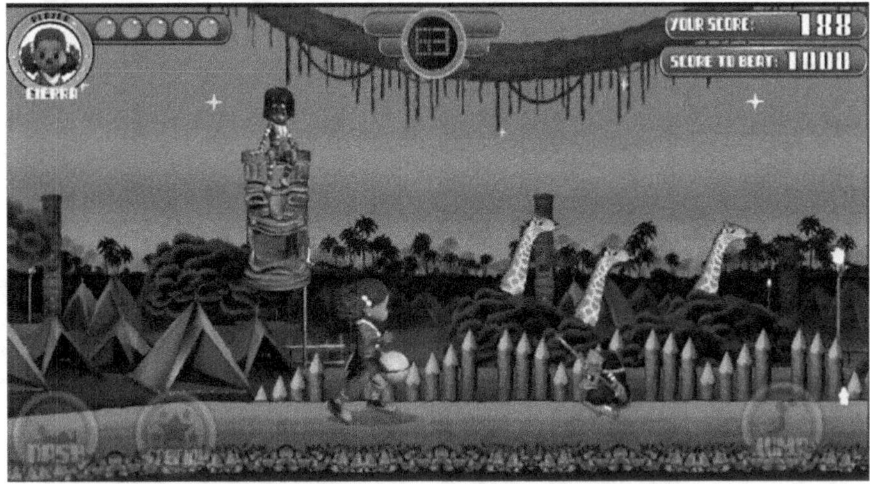

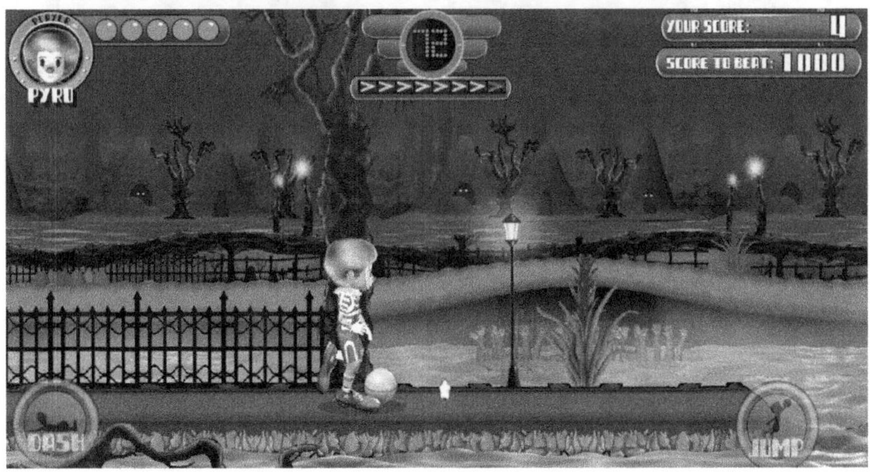

Super Stick Skirmish of Superb Scrappers

Released: 2008
Windows XP, VISTA, or 7, Windows 8
www.byond.com/games/MechaDestroyerJD/SuperStickSkirmishof
SuperbScrappers#

By: Mecha Destroyer JD
Memphis, TN

Super Stick Skirmish of Superb Scrappers is a competitive fighting game where you type to land blows on your opponent. You can play either against various levels of CPU or against another player online. There are scoreboards Medals aka achievements/trophies on the game's website.

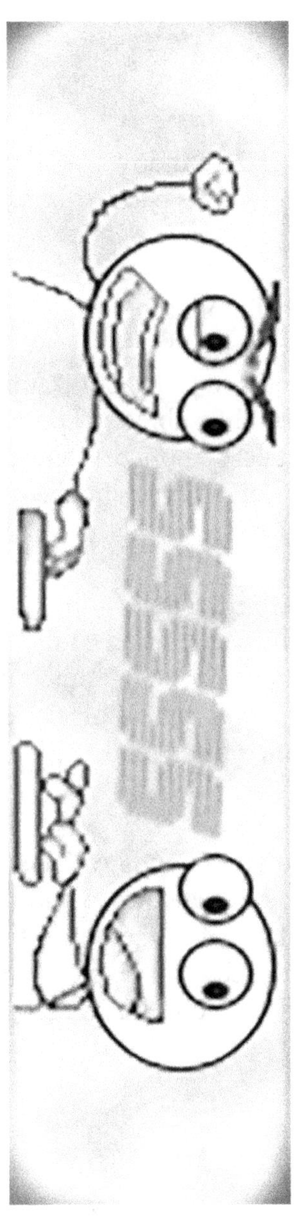

Systemic Lives

Released: 2020
Windows XP, VISTA, or 7, Windows 8, Windows 10
https://digitaldaydream.itch.io/systemic-lives

By: Digital Daydream
Raleigh-Durham, North Carolina

When we created this game in June 2020, Conversation in the United States was dominated by the subject of police brutality. However, hidden beneath the issues of police violence lies a larger web of racial disparities and systematic racism that affects black lives every day.

This project attempts to illustrate some of these disparities by simulating a series of lives according to the player's choices. Using real data, the game will determine the outcome of chosen events for groups of white people and groups of black people - side by side. As more and more lives are simulated, hidden imbalances become transparent.

Systemic Lives will evolve as you play. The conclusion of the game relieves the player of individual choice and forces them to simulate lives at scale. The final act of the removes the names and bodies of the lives simulated and leaves the player with raw data, which matches the research data used to make this game.

Systemic Lives

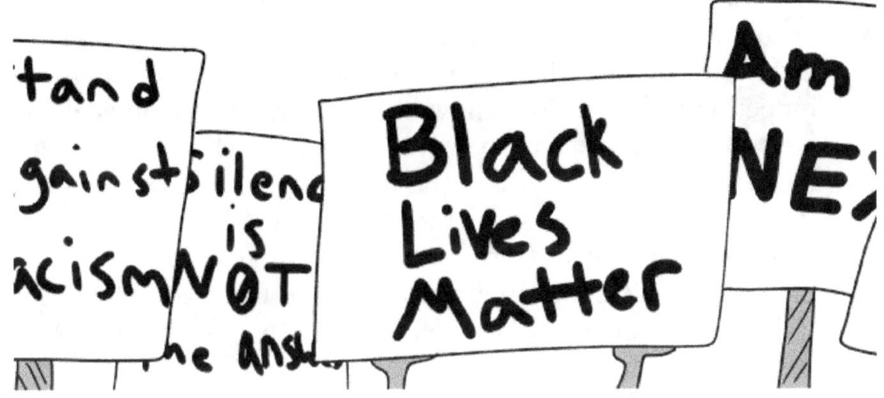

The 1998 Deck
Released: 2015
Card Game
The1998deck.com

By: Ordinary Genius Llc.
Georgia

Hip hop is a competitive sport'. So they say. So is poker, spades and even a rigorous game of Go Fish. The design of a modern playing card is meant to mimic the figures of war. The 1998 deck marries the competition of the card game with the classic Hip Hop beefs of the 1990s. 1998 marked an expansive movement in hip hop so many artists had blockbuster successes and huge album releases that year. That being said, that year was chosen as the marker for who was chosen to be in the deck. Hence the name of the series. The deck contains rappers (dead or alive) who were the titans of industry in that time period. It gives cards players (especially spades players) an opportunity to play cards with the 'Gods of Rap'. The game therefore becomes an emotional investment. Not only does the player feel the excitement of the game, but they play alongside some of their favorite artists. Kings and Queens who look like them, share their lineage and culture and reminds them what genius looks like when it comes from a tough beginnings. It's quite beautiful.

The Undefeated:
https://theundefeated.com/whhw/your-spades-game-needs-an-upgrade/

http://voyageatl.com/interview/check-khia-jacksons-artwork/

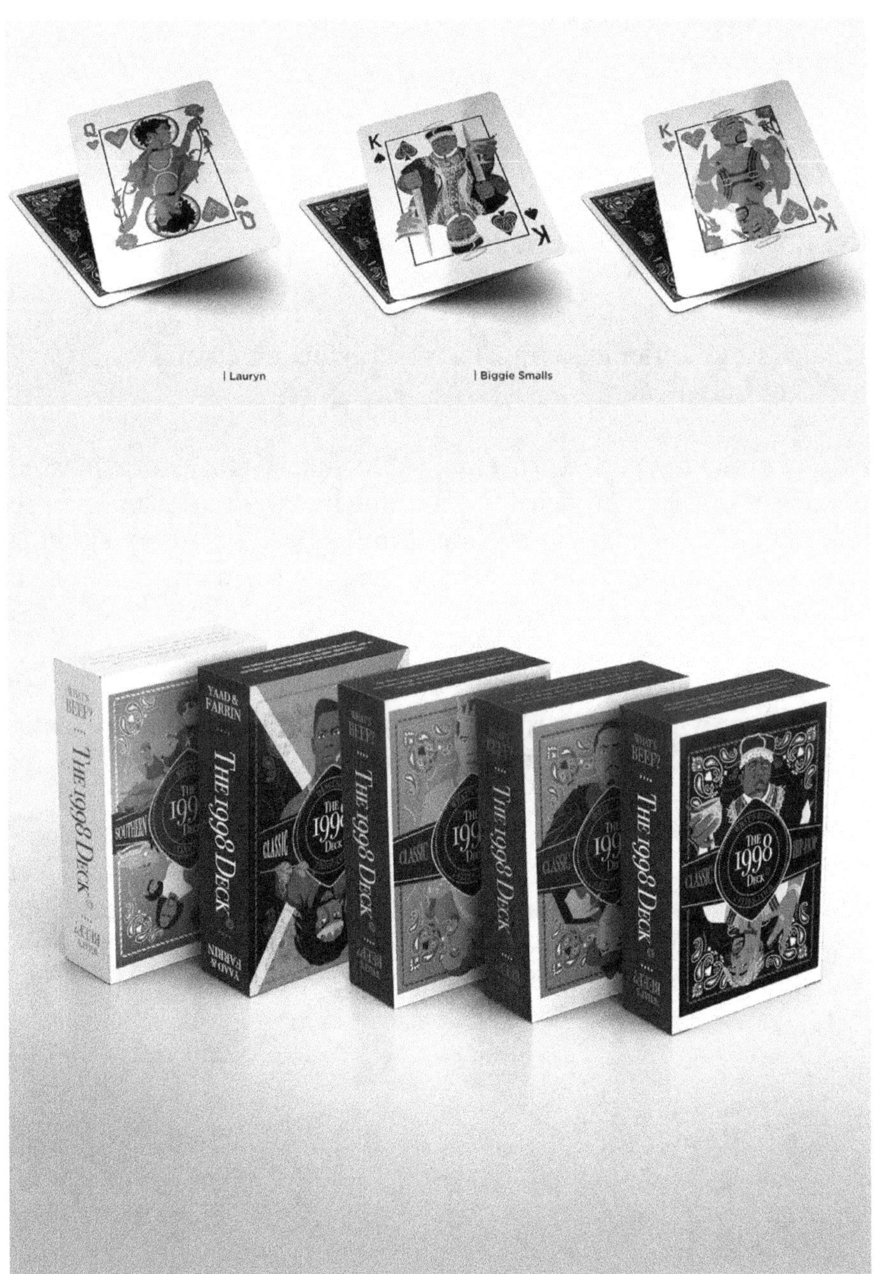

| Lauryn

| Biggie Smalls

The Ice Cold RPG

Released: 2020
Analog Role-Playing Game
https://www.amazon.com/Ice-Cold-RPG-Balogun-
Ojetade/dp/B08DBYMR74

By: Roaring Lions Productions
Atlanta, Georgia

Join Ice Cold Carter in saving the world again in the wacky way only Ice Cold Carter can.

Be a world-class martial artist that works for the most world classed of the world class martial artists. But watch out! You don't wanna be beaten by an Alien Ninja--an Alien Ninja's beat will turn you into a Zombie Ninja faster than a zombie's BITE will turn you into a plain ol' zombie.

Survive the dangers lurking out there--and Ice Cold Carter's insatiable craving for cheesecake and you just might become a Chief Supreme Grandmaster yourself one day, many years from now, in your dreams.

The ICE COLD RPG is a role playing game powered by an innovative card-based mechanic that provides fast and cinematic fun for players 13 years old or older (even a little younger if you're a cool parent... or an irresponsible one; either works).

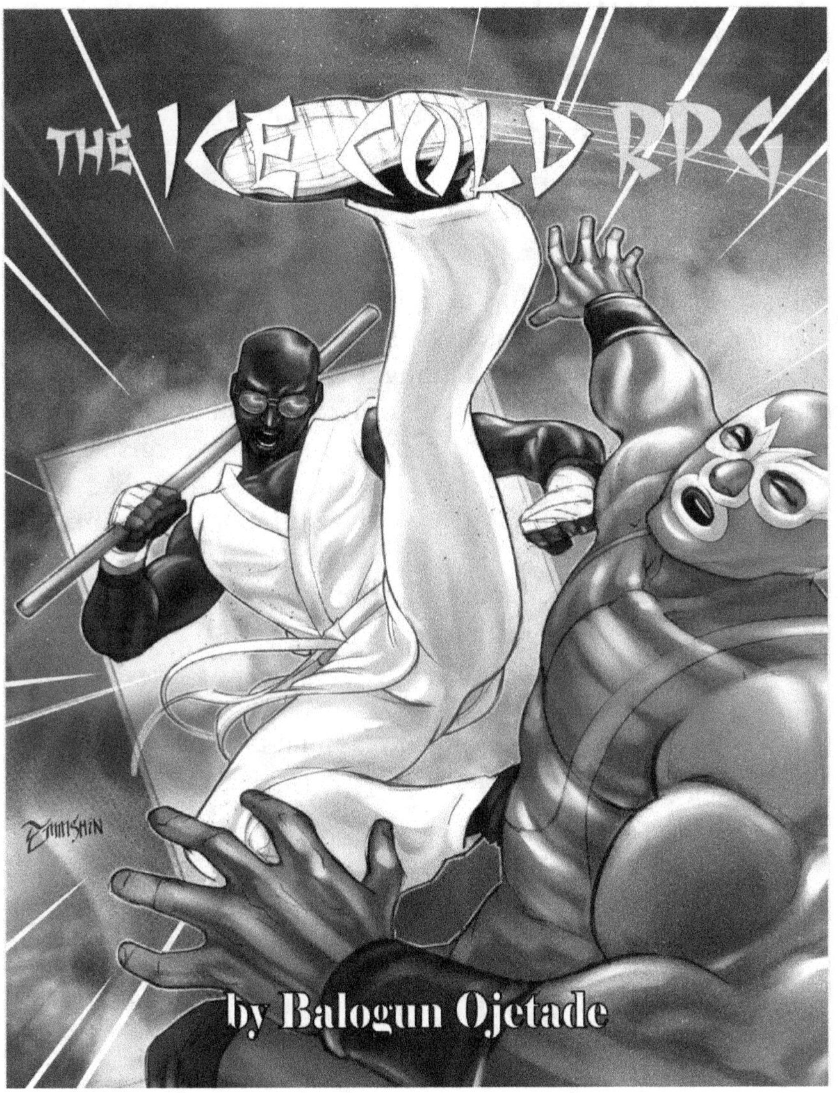

THE ICE COLD RPG
by Balogun Ojetade

The Run Around

Released: 2021
Board, Card or other analog game
https://ithrivegames.org/ithrive-research/juvenile-justice-research/

By: iThrive Games' SEED Institute
Boston, MA

The Run Around is a game designed by youth who have lived experience in the justice system or Department of Youth Services (or both). It is designed to (1) highlight inequities of those systems in supporting the mental health and thriving of youth of color, and (2) dismantle unjust systems. The Run Around represents some of the thoughts, feelings, and choices the youth designers had while incarcerated or on probation or parole—frustration, boredom, lack of purpose, and absence of agency. The game is a tool to raise awareness of these experiences and initiate conversations about systems change for social justice.

https://www.ludogogy.co.uk/article/imagining-a-better-world-game-design-with-and-for-teens/

Black Game Studies

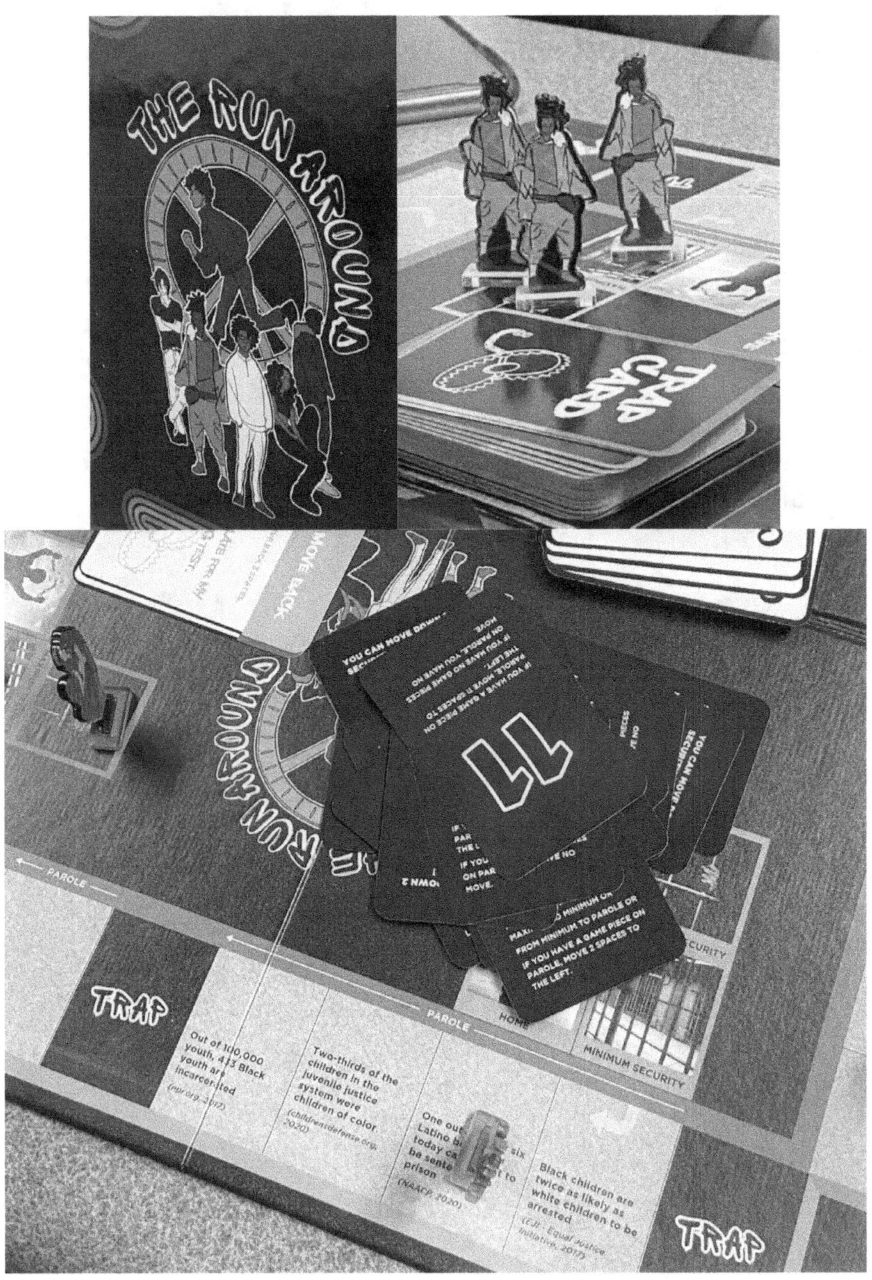

The Ultimate Clap Back
Released: 2017
Board, Card or other analog game
www.theultimateclapback.com

By: Mot & Dot LLC
New York, New York

The Ultimate Clap Back is not your parents' night-in of playing pinochle and spades. The Ultimate Clap Back is a fast-paced game of wordplay. With just the right amount of
sarcasm, snark and shade, this card game is bound to shock and keep you laughing
for hours!

Press:
https://www.theroot.com/the-ultimate-clap-back-does-it-for-the-culture-1828473052

https://www.mic.com/articles/181283/4-indie-games-from-developers-of-color-that-you-should-check-out-now#.enjXuZpGa

https://venturebeat.com/2017/06/27/game-devs-of-color-expo-highlights-the-diversity-already-in-gaming/"

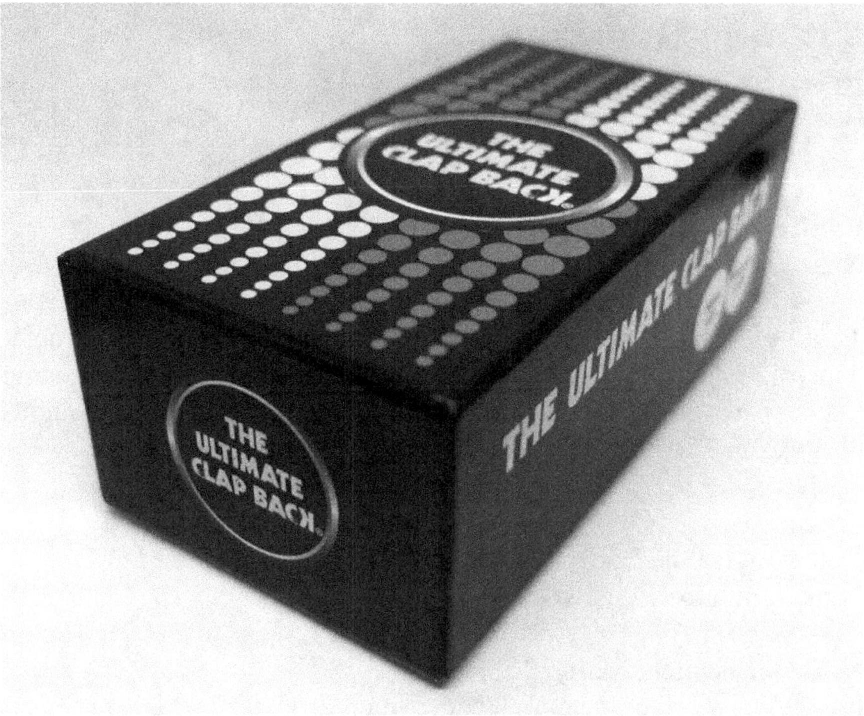

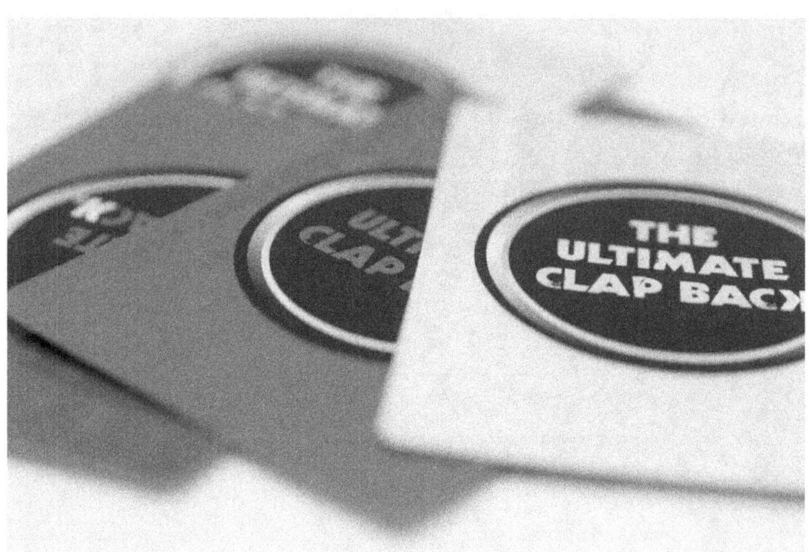
THE
ULTIMATE
CLAP BACK.

THE
ULTIMATE
CLAP BACK.

THE ULTIMATE CLAP BACK

THE
ULTIMATE
CLAP BACK

Trading Races

Released: 2017
Board, Card or other analog game
www.tradingracesgame.com

By: Kenyatta Forbes
Chicago, IL

Trading Races facilitates lively conversation around racial constructs and what it means to be Black — all through a card game that's part party game, part educational, and 100% thought-provoking. The rules are simple. The discussions won't be.

Press:
Vice News, June 2019:
https://youtu.be/FUy4wC2k-WI

NPR Codeswitch, March 2016
https://www.npr.org/sections/codeswitch/2017/03/16/520411515/who-s-the-blackest-of-them-all-a-new-card-game-seeks-to-find-out

Chicago Tribune:
https://www.chicagotribune.com/lifestyles/holiday/gift-guide/ct-gift-guide-blm-black-owned-1122-20201102-ounwtreckzcrjfuyhh3lblqml4-list.html

Essence Magazine
https://www.essence.com/culture/black-card-revoked-trading-races/?iid=sr-link1

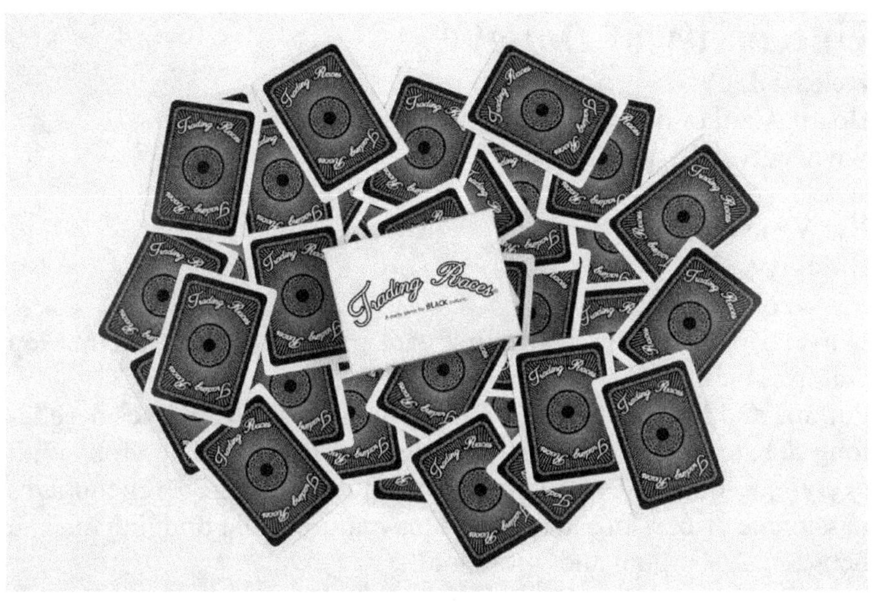

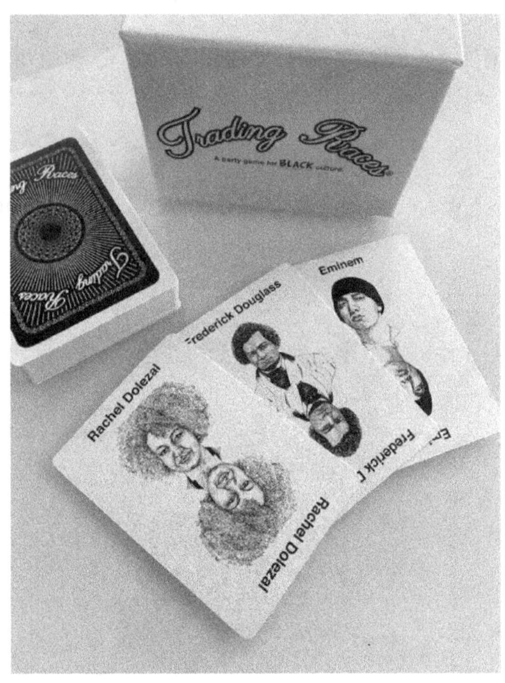

Rachel Dolezal
Frederick Douglass
Eminem

University of Dope™

Released: 2016
Board, Card or other analog game
www.universityofdope.com

By: Vance Hall LLC
Brooklyn, NY

University of Dope™ is the first card game dedicated to Hip Hop culture since 2016. Created by two dynamic lady "MCs", A.V. Perkins and Marian Andoh, University of DopeTM revives decade-long debates about the most controversial topics in Hip Hop. With every question and challenge, University of Dope™ encourages passionate discussions about Hip Hop culture while bridging the gap between new school and old school.

Huffington Post:
https://www.huffpost.com/entry/marian-andoh-and-av-perkins-challenge-your-hip-hop_b_59e5e421e4b08c75593ce656

Essence Magazine
https://www.essence.com/lifestyle/black-owned-culture-card-games/

Esquire Magazine:
https://www.esquire.com/lifestyle/g1943/gifts-for-men/"

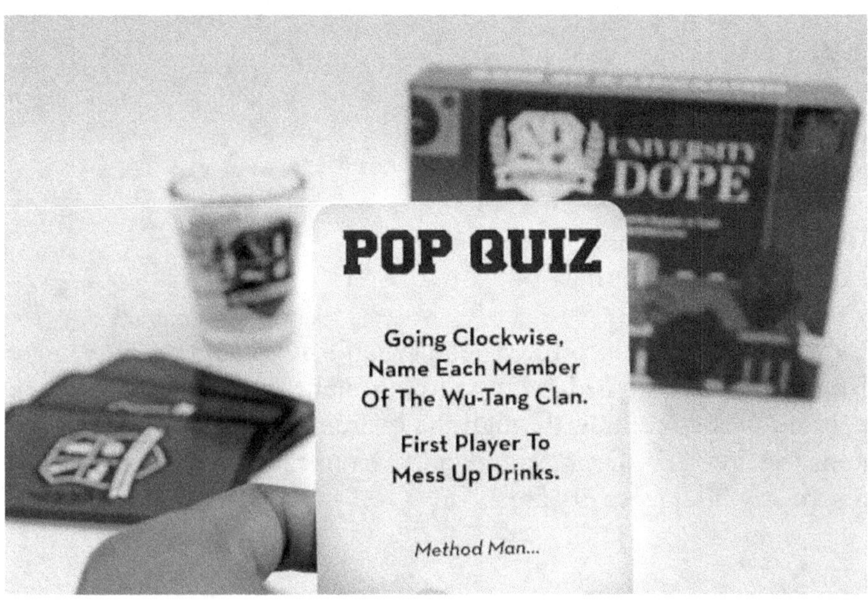
POP QUIZ

Going Clockwise,
Name Each Member
Of The Wu-Tang Clan.

First Player To
Mess Up Drinks.

Method Man...

UNIVERSITY
DOPE

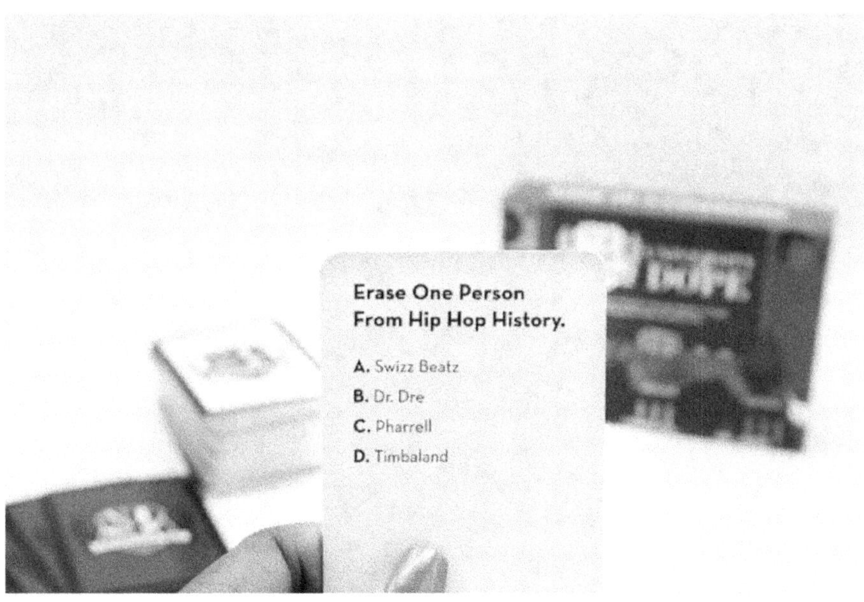
Erase One Person
From Hip Hop History.

A. Swizz Beatz
B. Dr. Dre
C. Pharrell
D. Timbaland

UnStuck

Released: 2021
Mac OS, Windows XP, VISTA, or 7, Windows 8
https://www.instagram.com/unstuckgame/

By: Indefinite Village
Los Angeles, California

Exhausted from their former friend group's microaggressions, Jaime stumbles upon Aligned, a free virtual telehealth therapy for Black people. While working through the exercises presented to them by their therapist, Dr. Dean, Jaime works to reframe their thoughts and discover who they really are.

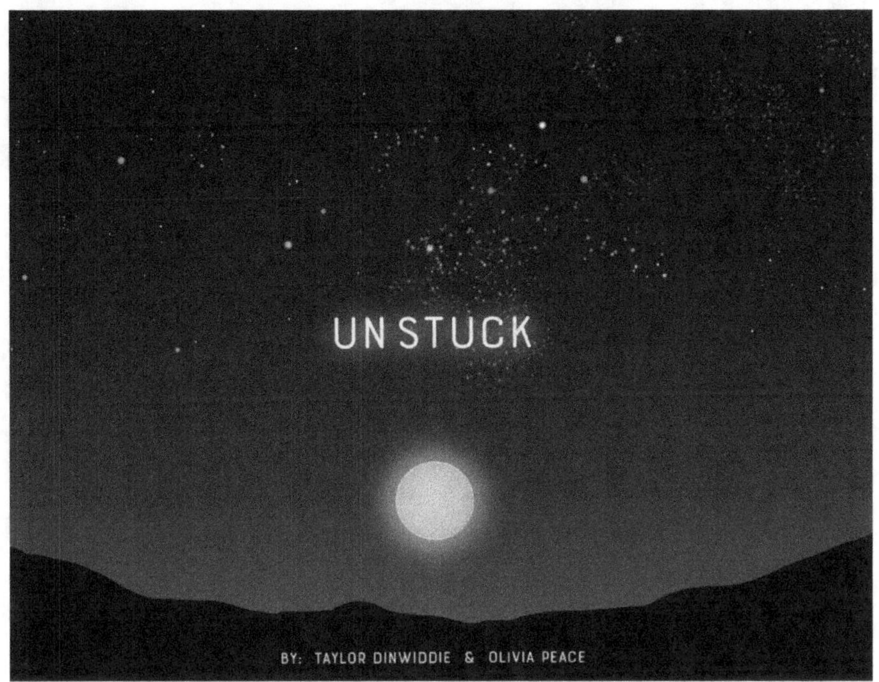
UN STUCK
BY: TAYLOR DINWIDDIE & OLIVIA PEACE

When I Get Free (WIGF)
Released: 2019
Mobile: iOS
kenegutv.com/home/games/

By: The Books Of Egu
Los Angeles, California

When I Get Free is a series of fictional video games and interactive content inspired by the New Testament. It takes players on a hands on visual and musical adventure filled with adrenaline, puzzling mysteries, and engaging animations.

We follow Jon, Peta and Judah (futuristic re-imaginations of John the Baptist, Peter and Judas) who are wrongfully imprisoned and banished to the dystopian city of Nemean. Together, they develop an elaborate plan to escape toward freedom and the promise of a savior who awaits on the other side.

Breaking out of a city wide prison won't be easy. No inmate has ever escaped the high level security around Nemean. However, with the annual Nemean Games happening in town, where inmates compete for their freedom, everybody's attention will be focused on that. John, Peta and Judah see this as their only chance to escape. Users will play various chapters as each character, completing different tasks that take you on a challenging journey filled with thrilling car chases to tricky puzzles to intense fight scenes and more. What are you willing to do to get free?

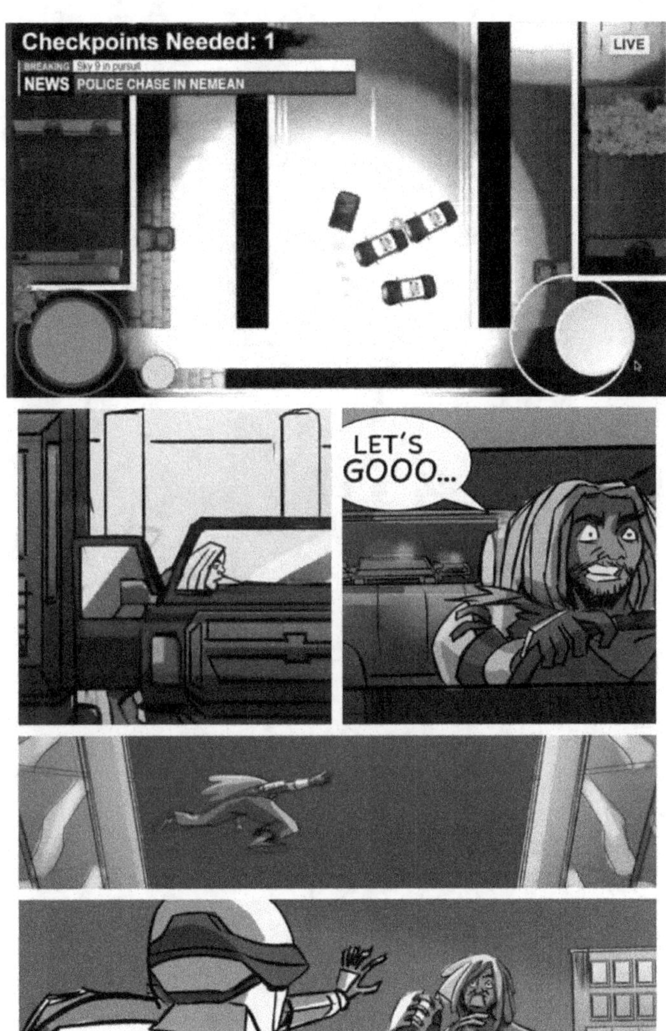
Checkpoints Needed: 1
LIVE
BREAKING Sky 9 in pursuit
NEWS POLICE CHASE IN NEMEAN
LET'S GOOO...

■Black Game Studies

The ETC Press was founded in 2005 under the direction of Dr. Drew Davidson, the Director of Carnegie Mellon University's Entertainment Technology Center (ETC), as an open access, digital-first publishing house.

What does all that mean?

The ETC Press publishes three types of work:peer-reviewed work (research-based books, textbooks, academic journals, conference proceedings), general audience work (trade nonfiction, singles, Well Played singles), and research and white papers
The common tie for all of these is a focus on issues related to entertainment technologies as they are applied across a variety of fields.

Our authors come from a range of backgrounds. Some are traditional academics. Some are practitioners. And some work in between. What ties them all together is their ability to write about the impact of emerging technologies and its significance in society.

To distinguish our books, the ETC Press has five imprints:
- ETC Press: our traditional academic and peer-reviewed publications;
- ETC Press: Single: our short "why it matters" books that are roughly 8,000-25,000 words;
- ETC Press: Signature: our special projects, trade books, and other curated works that exemplify the best work being done;
- ETC Press: Report: our white papers and reports produced by practitioners or academic researchers working in conjunction with partners; and
- ETC Press: Student: our work with undergraduate and graduate students

In keeping with that mission, the ETC Press uses emerging technologies to design all of our books and Lulu, an on-demand publisher, to distribute our e-books and print books through all the major retail chains, such as Amazon, Barnes & Noble, Kobo, and

Apple, and we work with The Game Crafter to produce tabletop games.

We don't carry an inventory ourselves. Instead, each print book is created when somebody buys a copy.

Since the ETC Press is an open-access publisher, every book, journal, and proceeding is available as a free download. We're most interested in the sharing and spreading of ideas. We also have an agreement with the Association for Computing Machinery (ACM) to list ETC Press publications in the ACM Digital Library. Authors retain ownership of their intellectual property. We release all of our books, journals, and proceedings under one of two

Creative Commons licenses:
•   Attribution-NoDerivativeWorks-NonCommercial: This license allows for published works to remain intact, but versions can be created; or
•   Attribution-NonCommercial-ShareAlike: This license allows for authors to retain editorial control of their creations while also encouraging readers to collaboratively rewrite content.

This is definitely an experiment in the notion of publishing, and we invite people to participate. We are exploring what it means to "publish" across multiple media and multiple versions. We believe this is the future of publication, bridging virtual and physical media with fluid versions of publications as well as enabling the creative blurring of what constitutes reading and writing.

www.ingramcontent.com/pod-product-compliance
Lightning Source LLC
Chambersburg PA
CBHW061755250726
48657CB00001B/136